Kingdom Come Leadership

Inspiring Your Church Toward Spiritual Maturity

by Bill Simpson

Bill's additional books, podcast, and blog can be found on his website: www.BillSimpson.org

Cover Design: Todd Phelps

DEDICATION

This book is dedicated to all of the pastors, bishops, missionaries, evangelists, elders, deacons, ministry directors, and church leaders all around the world who work diligently to advance Jesus' kingdom. Because we are held to a higher degree of accountability regarding how we lead God's people, I pray this book will bring you encouragement and clarity in your *responsibility to equip God's people to do his work and build up the church, the body of Christ.* Ephesians 4:12 HCSB

CHAPTERS

CHAPTER 1 – YOUR LEADERSHIP PRIORITIES

God has called you to an enormous task.

Regardless of whether you're a senior pastor or an elder or deacon, our Father has called you to lead those you serve towards spiritual maturity. In his final charge to the elders of the Ephesian church, Paul gave them a momentous directive: *Pay careful attention to yourselves and to all the flock in which the Holy Spirit has made you overseers, to care for the church of God, which he obtained with his own blood* (Acts 20:28). Peter gave a similar charge to church leaders to *shepherd the flock of God that is among you, exercising oversight, not under compulsion, but willingly, as God would have you; not for shameful gain, but eagerly; not domineering over those in your charge, but being examples to the flock* (1 Peter 5:-3). The verb translated in Acts 20:8 "to care" is the same word in Peter's passage to "shepherd". It's a common biblical metaphor that obviously means to lead, protect, defend, feed, and nurture. And Paul, from his preeminent passage about the purpose of church, calls for leaders to *equip the saints for the work of ministry, for building up the body of Christ, until we all attain to the unity of the faith and of the knowledge of the Son of God, to mature manhood, to the measure of the stature of the fullness of Christ* (Ephesians 4:12-13).

You understand this high calling. You have likely quivered in your boots at this high calling our Father in the heavens has placed on you. You want nothing more than to help people grow in their dedication to Jesus and their dependence on his Spirit. And, you have a million things you feel you need to accomplish. You face new pressures and challenges every day. Leading your church or ministry organization can be all-consuming. Let's face it, you often feel completely overwhelmed, and you're not sure what to prioritize. So, what exactly should you be doing to properly shepherd God's flock entrusted to your care? What are the key, mission-critical tasks that will build your church up in unity and maturity? What should take priority over all the other to-dos on your list that are clamoring for immediate attention?

Let's consider how the Kingdom's two greatest leaders prioritized their responsibilities.

The Greatest Leaders

Jesus the Christ, the Son of the Most High God, is certainly the preeminent leader; unlike anyone the world has ever known. He is unsurpassed and incomparable. And it can be very intimidating for a mere mortal to try to imitate the leadership of King Jesus. It is my deep conviction that God's second greatest leader was the Apostle Paul, and we can most definitely lead those entrusted to our care in the same way Paul led those under his spiritual guidance.

After his conversion, Paul was instrumental in leading thousands to believe in Jesus Christ as he and his team birthed churches throughout the Roman Empire. As a writer, Paul's influence is undeniable. His Spirit-inspired letters have had immeasurable impact on more than a billion people through the centuries, and they've been translated into more than 1,500 unique languages.

Therefore, as the leaders of God's people, shouldn't we be taking our leadership cues from Jesus and Paul? Imitating these two great leaders will position you to have the maximum Kingdom influence on everyone in your church or organization. Let's consider how each prioritized their days.

Prayer is Leadership

How did Jesus and Paul live out their leadership roles within their relationship to the Father? How did they become God's greatest leaders? Through constant communion with their Father. They spoke with him nonstop. Prayer was not a religious duty. Prayer was their lifeline because prayer is simply talking with our Father in the heavens about everything and everyone important to us and to him. As in every significant relationship we have, regular conversations are natural and essential. We simply can't have a close relationship if we don't regularly communicate. The closer the relationship, the more frequent and personal the conversations will be. The more we converse with our Father, the more powerful and effective our influence will be.

Jesus regularly left the disciples to be alone with his Father in prayer. Whether it was on a mountain, in the wilderness, or in some other desolate place, Jesus spent hours talking with his Father. That's part of what he is doing even now. The Bible tells us that Jesus continually intercedes for his followers (Romans 8:34 and Hebrews 7:25). Try to picture Jesus talking to his Father about that current situation weighing so heavily on you. He knows the pressures and challenges you are facing, and he is constantly speaking with his Father about you and your leadership responsibilities. What do you think he's asking his Father to do, specifically? Take a few moments and think about that. What is Jesus' perspective on your immediate ministry challenge?

You're not surprised how much Jesus prayed during his life on earth. We expect that from him. But can you and I truly pray as the Son of God did? Can we regularly pull all-nighters conversing with our heavenly Father? Probably not. You may want to. I wish I had that in me. However, we will never know the intimacy shared between the Son and Father, at least not on this side of eternity. So, thinking we can imitate Jesus' leadership impact according to how he prayed is probably out of reach for most of us.

Therefore, we need someone we can more closely identify with, who shares our limitations. If we're going to lead in such a way as to produce the kind of fruit that honors our Father, we need a mentor. We need someone we can both emulate in his leadership and his praying. We need a coach and a guide we can relate to, who shared similar challenges and setbacks.

Leaning into Paul

The man we can learn to most emulate is, in my opinion, the second greatest leader God has given to this world, Saul of Tarsus, the Apostle Paul. Remember, Saul was his Hebrew name, and Paul was his Roman name. Since he was a Jewish, Roman citizen, he used both names depending on the context (Acts 13:9). Because his ministry was primarily to non-Jews, Luke used his Roman name throughout most of Acts, especially from chapter 14 onward.

A practical leadership question is: How did Paul spend the majority of his time? What were his daily priorities? How did he lead his own team, while having so much influence on multiple churches? Realize Paul always worked with a small group of revolving co-ministers as he traveled throughout the Roman world. He not only influenced thousands with his teaching, he was continually mentoring those who traveled with him.

So, two critically important questions are: What did his daily to-do list look like, and how did he prioritize those activities? He certainly spent a lot of time teaching and preaching the fantastic reality of forgiveness from sins through faith in Jesus Christ. And in some towns, he spent time making tents to help fund the ministry. But *what* was his daily priority? Every great leader has to prioritize their time. How did Paul balance mentoring his team members with reaching the lost and equipping the found?

He prayed. He taught his team how to pray. They prayed together. They prayed for each other. They prayed for all the believers in every church. They prayed for the lost, the chosen, and for government leaders.

They prayed daily, consistently, and fervently. They prayed for the Kingdom to come.

Praying for the churches was Paul's highest priority. Teaching his team members how to pray was next on his list. From reading his letters in the New Testament, we get the idea he led his team in regular times of prayer for the believers in the various churches every day, and possibly, multiple times throughout each day and night. Let's take a look at how Paul described his and his team's prayer priority to better understand his commitment to, and reliance upon, asking his Father for help.

Paul's Prayer Priority

At least 13 of the New Testament's 27 letters were authored by the Apostle Paul. There is ongoing debate as to the authorship of the letter to the Hebrews, so Paul's total may even be 14. In 11 of those 13 letters, Paul described his prayer priority, detailing how he and his team prayed for the believers in each church. As you read these passages, underline key phrases about prayer that stand out to you.

To the **Roman** church he wrote;

1:9 For God is my witness, whom I serve with my spirit in the gospel of his Son, that without ceasing I mention you 10 always in my prayers, asking that somehow by God's will I may now at last succeed in coming to you.

10:1 Brothers, my heart's desire and prayer to God for them is that they may be saved.

To the **Corinthian** church Paul wrote in his second letter;

7 But we pray to God that you may not do wrong—not that we may appear to have met the test, but that you may do what is right, though we may seem to have failed. 8 For we cannot do anything against the truth, but only for the truth. 9 For we are glad when we are weak and you are strong. Your restoration is what we pray for.

Paul spent more time in Ephesus than anywhere else, so he knew these believers extremely well. To the **Ephesian** church he wrote;

1:15 For this reason, because I have heard of your faith in the Lord Jesus and your love toward all the saints, 16 I do not cease to give thanks for you, remembering you in my prayers,

3:14 For this reason, I bow my knees before the Father, from whom every family in heaven and on earth is named,

Paul was especially inspired by the Philippian church's continual demonstration of faith through their love and sacrificial giving (see 2 Corinthians 8:1-5). Notice how the Apostle prayed for the **Philippian** church;

1:3 I thank my God in all my remembrance of you, 4 always in every prayer of mine for you all making my prayer with joy, 5 because of your partnership in the gospel from the first day until now.

1:9 And it is my prayer that your love may abound more and more, with knowledge and all discernment,

Paul's letters to the Ephesian, Philippian, and Colossian churches were written during his imprisonment in Rome. They carry similarities but also emphasize unique aspects of faith in Christ. Paul and his team, especially a man named Epaphras, prayed continuously for these churches. To the **Colossians** he was inspired by God to write;

1:3 We always thank God, the Father of our Lord Jesus Christ, when we pray for you,

1:9 And so, from the day we heard, we have not ceased to pray for you, asking that you may be filled with the knowledge of his will in all spiritual wisdom and understanding,

4:12 Epaphras, who is one of you, a servant of Christ Jesus, greets you, always struggling on your behalf in his prayers, that you may stand mature and fully assured in all the will of God.

The churches in the cities of Philippi, Thessalonica, and Berea were all located in the region called Macedonia. These three churches were birthed during Paul's second missionary journey (Acts 16-17). Read how he emphasized prayer in both of his letters addressed to the **Thessalonians**;

1 Thessalonians 1:2 We give thanks to God always for all of you, constantly mentioning you in our prayers, 3 remembering before our God and Father your work of faith and labor of love and steadfastness of hope in our Lord Jesus Christ.

3:9 For what thanksgiving can we return to God for you, for all the joy that we feel for your sake before our God, 10 as we pray most earnestly night and day that we may see you face to face and supply what is lacking in your faith?

2 Thessalonians 1:11 *To this end we always pray for you, that our God may make you worthy of his calling and may fulfill every resolve for good and every work of faith by his power, ¹² so that the name of our Lord Jesus may be glorified in you, and you in him, according to the grace of our God and the Lord Jesus Christ.*

Paul also wrote three letters that are referred to as "pastoral letters." Two of these letters were written to the young evangelist, Timothy, and one to Paul's faithful companion, Titus. Timothy traveled with Paul throughout most of his second and third missionary journeys (Acts 17:14-15; 18:5; 19:22 and 20:4). Titus apparently traveled with Paul during the same timeframe as did Timothy. Paul gave Titus the mission-critical task of appointing elders in many of the newly birthed churches. There is no doubt that Paul continually prayed for Titus even though he does not mention it in his short letter to his trusted minister. No doubt, Paul prayed for Titus in the same way he prayed for all of those who traveled with him, as he expressed in his second letter to **Timothy**.

2:3 *I thank God whom I serve, as did my ancestors, with a clear conscience, as I remember you constantly in my prayers night and day.*

Finally, Paul shared with his friend Philemon how he constantly prayed for him. It's helpful to note that **Philemon** was a member of the church in Colossae.

⁴ I thank my God always when I remember you in my prayers, ⁵ because I hear of your love and of the faith that you have toward the Lord Jesus and for all the saints, ⁶ and I pray that the sharing of your faith may become effective for the full knowledge of every good thing that is in us for the sake of Christ.

Take a moment to re-read those passages again and focus on what you underlined. What is your Father speaking to you?

Is there any doubt about what head lined the Apostle's daily to-do list? He and his team members continually prayed for the believers in the various churches and for their co-workers, both night and day.

Can you do that? Can you commit to praying diligently for those you shepherd? You may be thinking, "I doubt it." I don't blame you. As a missionary and a senior pastor, I often lacked Paul's commitment to praying for those I led. Of course, I prayed for them, but it could in no way be compared to how Paul prayed or how he taught his team members to pray.

So, what do you and I need to do to ramp up our commitment to prioritizing prayer to resemble Paul's? First, obedience to God's word is how we show Jesus we truly love him. "*If you love me, you will keep my commandments*" declared our Lord and Savior. If you're not willing to obey *all* of Jesus' teachings, which means the entirety of the Old and New Testaments, then go find another religion to follow. That's a little harsh. But seriously, we must wrap our hearts and heads around the fact that obeying all of the Bible is not an option. Obedience is to be our highest goal. And obedience in prayer is how we strengthen our dependence on our heavenly Father. As we all know, regular communication is essential to every healthy relationship, especially ours with God.

What Paul Taught About Prayer

In the same way Paul prayed, he also instructed the believers in those churches to be constant in prayer, just as Jesus taught (Matthew 6:6-8 and 7:7-11; and Luke 11:9-13). Maybe the best-known instruction from Paul about persistence in praying is found in 1 Thessalonians 5:17 – *Pray without ceasing.* The original Greek adverb means continually, unintermittedly, and incessantly. The New Living Translation worded it this way; *Never stop praying.*

Read the following additional instructions from the Apostle to the various churches, and to Timothy, about how believers are to pray. Again, as you read, underline the key phrases that stand out to you.

Romans

12:12 Rejoice in hope, be patient in tribulation, be constant in prayer.

15:30 I appeal to you, brothers, by our Lord Jesus Christ and by the love of the Spirit, to strive together with me in your prayers to God on my behalf,

1 Corinthians (regarding intimacy in marriage)

7:5 Do not deprive one another, except perhaps by agreement for a limited time, that you may devote yourselves to prayer; but then come together again, so that Satan may not tempt you because of your lack of self-control.

2 Corinthians

1:11 You also must help us by prayer, so that many will give thanks on our behalf for the blessing granted us through the prayers of many.

9:14 while they long for you and pray for you, because of the surpassing grace of God upon you.

Ephesians

6:16 In all circumstances take up the shield of faith, with which you can extinguish all the flaming darts of the evil one; 17 and take the helmet of salvation, and the sword of the Spirit, which is the word of God, 18 praying at all times in the Spirit, with all prayer and supplication. To that end, keep alert with all perseverance, making supplication for all the saints, 19 and also for me, that words may be given to me in opening my mouth boldly to proclaim the mystery of the gospel, for which I am an ambassador in chains, that I may declare it boldly, as I ought to speak.

Philippians

1:19 for I know that through your prayers and the help of the Spirit of Jesus Christ this will turn out for my deliverance,

4:4 Rejoice in the Lord always; again I say, rejoice. 5 Let your reasonableness be known to everyone. The Lord is at hand; 6 do not be anxious about anything, but in everything by prayer and supplication with thanksgiving let your requests be made known to God. 7 And the peace of God, which surpasses all understanding, will guard your hearts and your minds in Christ Jesus.

Colossians

4:2 Continue steadfastly in prayer, being watchful in it with thanksgiving. 3 At the same time, pray also for us, that God may open to us a door for the word, to declare the mystery of Christ, on account of which I am in prison — 4 that I may make it clear, which is how I ought to speak.

1 Thessalonians

5:16 Rejoice always, 17 pray without ceasing, 18 give thanks in all circumstances; for this is the will of God in Christ Jesus for you.

5:25 Brothers, pray for us.

2 Thessalonians

3:1 Finally, brothers, pray for us, that the word of the Lord may speed ahead and be honored, as happened among you, 2 and that we may be delivered from wicked and evil men. For not all have faith.

1 Timothy

2:1 First of all, then, I urge that supplications, prayers, intercessions, and thanksgivings be made for all people, 2 for kings and all who are in high positions, that we may lead a peaceful and quiet life, godly and dignified in every way.

2:8 I desire then that in every place the men should pray, lifting holy hands without anger or quarreling;

5:5 She who is truly a widow, left all alone, has set her hope on God and continues in supplications and prayers night and day, 6 but she who is self-indulgent is dead even while she lives.

Philemon

1:22 At the same time, prepare a guest room for me, for I am hoping that through your prayers I will be graciously given to you.

Read what you underlined from these passages. What is God impressing on your heart and mind about how you and your church are to pray?

I hope it's not guilt, but it may well be. It's difficult to read these exhortations without feeling guilty because you don't consistently pray that way. But you can. That's the purpose of this book – to help you grow in your confidence that you and your fellow leaders can pray like Paul and his team. Because your Father's desire is to advance his kingdom through your leadership, he wants you to learn how to pray in a similar manner to Paul.

The power of prayer is undeniable. Our call to pray is unquestionable. Our direct access to the Father is inescapable. God's unequivocal desire is that we ask for his help in everything and with everyone. So why in the world is praying such a challenge for the vast majority of Kingdom leaders? We must take a deeper dive into the Scriptures to learn the answer.

Without Ceasing?

What does it mean to *continue steadfastly in prayer* and to *pray without ceasing*? Did Paul intend all of Jesus' followers to pray 24/7? Or did he intend just a select few ministers should develop an effective, ongoing, conversational prayer with their Father similar to he and his team members practiced? Is this command just for pastors, bishops, and church elders? Through the inspiration of the Spirit of Jesus, Paul encouraged all believers to practice an on-going conversation with the Father. But this type of praying must be modeled by leaders first and foremost.

What do you do when something good, funny, or bad happens to you? Do you fire off a text to your spouse or a close friend? If you need someone's help, you likely text them. If you need information, you send a text or email. I've stood in the grocery store countless times texting my wife because I couldn't remember what I needed to pick up on the way home. Can I get an "Amen?"

Praying to our Father in the heavens is similar. You will benefit tremendously, as will those you lead, as you begin to develop the habit of praying as frequently as you text or email. Your leadership influence will greatly increase as you speak with your Father throughout the day about the people you lead, as the Spirit brings them to your mind, and through planned times of intercession.

In a previous pastorate, the elders and I decided to divide the church family evenly between the eight of us so we could collectively pray daily for everyone in our church family. We used the Kingdom Come Prayers that will be discussed throughout the remainder of this book, coupled with specific prayer requests of which we were aware. We pledged to one another to pray for those on our list at least once daily, with several times being preferred. The elders and I then communicated our commitment to the church family so they could be confident we were partnering with them in asking our Father to grow us all towards unity and maturity. This not only helped the congregation to understand more fully the role of an elder, it also inspired them to begin to pray similarly for their family members, friends, and small group members. The outcome was tangible.

Kingdom Life is Tough

Before we move onto how to pray, let's remind ourselves why it's mission-critical for every Kingdom member living in this sin-saturated world.

Jesus said devotion to him is like taking the narrow way which is difficult to follow, and that only a few actually make it. That's tough to hear. But life on this earth as a believer is very challenging to do, especially following him faithfully. And it's getting more and more challenging. Jesus' followers are now in the overwhelming minority and are considered to be bigots, prejudice, judgmental, and homophobic. We must recognize how obeying Jesus is difficult to do. Experiencing these challenges should inspire us to seeking and asking and knocking, as we come to understand our desperate dependence on God. As a leader, you must realize how desperately dependent on the Lord those you influence truly are, even if they don't understand it. You can only maximize your Kingdom influence on your church family as you remain in desperate need of Jesus' help.

Luke wrote in Acts 14:22 that he, Paul, and the other members of their ministry team were committed to the ministry of *strengthening the souls of the disciples, encouraging them to continue in the faith, and saying that through many tribulations we must enter the kingdom of God*. This is your ministry too. For every person within your circle of influence, you have the high calling to strengthen and encourage them because life is hard. The most effective way of building them up in their faith is through asking the Father for his help, just as the Apostle Paul and his team continually did.

The Battle with Busy

We're all very busy, especially church leaders. The problems and trials your people have are never-ending. Although you know prayer is essential and powerful, it's still challenging to carve out significant time in your day to pray for your church family. There are so many other voices crying for your immediate attention.

For me, my lack of diligent intercession was due primarily to a lack of confidence. I doubted, by my very lack of interceding, that our Father would do what I asked because I really wasn't certain what I should be asking him to do. Can you relate? I lacked confidence my Father truly wanted to do what I was asking of him. And my church family was extremely diverse with a plethora of unique situations and setbacks. Each person was at a different place in their spiritual growth. How could I take the time to pray specifically for each of these individuals and families with any confidence that the time I spent praying would prove fruitful?

I began a journey of studying the Scriptures to find some answers. I wanted to believe Jesus' amazing promises about prayer in John 14-16. I wanted to understand what it means to pray "in his name" and to have his words "abide in" me, so whatever I asked I would receive. What did Jesus really intend when he promised if we would ask and keep asking, and seek and keep seeking, and knock and keep knocking, we would indeed be given what we ask, find what we are seeking, and walk through the doors we are banging on?

The Apostle John discovered it. Therefore, after following Jesus for more than 60 years and under the inspiration of the Holy Spirit he wrote: *And this is the confidence that we have toward him, that if we ask anything according to his will he hears us. And if we know that he hears us in whatever we ask, we know that we have the requests that we have asked of him* (1 John 5:14).

How could John write with such bold confidence about prayer? He understood the promise of our Lord Jesus that he spoke that holy Thursday night (John 14-17). John learned how to pray for the Kingdom to come, which is exactly what Paul and his teams did so fervently. Praying the way these apostles prayed is how you can maximize your leadership impact and advance the Kingdom in and through your church, the very work you were created in Christ to do.

The next chapter explores what Jesus meant when he instructed us to ask for *the Kingdom to come.*

CHAPTER 2 – THE KINGDOM COMES FIRST

Jesus' disciples, who became the Apostles, struggled with prayer just like we do. They had been following him more than two years when we read their request in Luke 11:1; *"Lord, teach us to pray, as John* (John the Baptist) *taught his disciples."* This question came after Jesus had returned from one of his long, intimate prayer times with his Father. Jesus left them to be alone in prayer on a regular basis, sometimes even through the night. After watching him pray for the past two plus years, they found the nerve to ask him to teach them how to pray in the same way.

Don't you know Jesus must have been thinking, "Finally, you ask!" As the master strategist, he developed his leadership team while he was revealing his divinity to them and the crowds through his teaching and miracles. Now was the moment for which he'd been waiting. The

Twelve were ready to learn how to pray to the Father. Jesus must have been ecstatic at their request.

How Jesus taught them is profound. His teaching holds the key for every leader in Christ's kingdom to understand fully what we need to know about prayer. He gave his leadership team exactly what they needed to be able to have the kind of kingdom impact they were called to have. His teaching will do the same for you.

The Follower's Prayer Outline

Luke 11:2-4 and Matthew 6:9-13 are referred to as "The Lord's Prayer". However, this is not the Lord's prayer at all. It is "The Followers' Prayer Outline" given to us by our Lord. When his disciples asked him to teach them how to pray, Jesus gave them, and us, a very detailed outline, or framework, for how to have rich conversations with God and to do so with unwavering confidence. Confidence in praying is the key to being diligent and constant in prayer. The outline is the pattern for all of his people to use when talking with the heavenly Father about all the things that concern both us and him. This outline is how we develop a powerful habit of engaging in rich, meaningful conversations with the God of the universe in longer times of praying, in text-prayers during the day, and in those heat-of-the-moment flare prayers.

However, the Church has been using this prayer outline incorrectly for centuries. There's no way Jesus meant for us to simply recite these specific words to God and think we've prayed. There are only 38 words in the original Greek. Reciting it at a normal pace will take you between 13-15 seconds. Was Jesus purpose to give us a prayer we could recite in 15 seconds? Was that his answer to his disciples request to teach them how to pray? Is he giving us just a few words to pray because we are such busy people? Not a chance.

So how do we build our confidence that we really do know what to ask of God? How do we reject the incessant desires of the "Me Monster" (I'm borrowing this phrase from comedian Brian Regan) within? You don't have to figure it out on your own. You don't have to wonder if you have it right. Jesus' words are like the Maps or Waze app on your phone, guiding you where you need to go. We must center our lives, and most definitely our conversations with God, on Jesus' teaching of how he instructed us to *order* our praying by using the Followers' Prayer Outline.

Going through the whole outline can take as little as a few minutes, or it can lead you into an hour or more of praying to the Father. But you can also jump into any of the five categories in the outline as a text-prayer or a flare prayer. The key to confidence in praying is to own the five categories and understand why Jesus gave us this framework. Read below the Follower's Prayer Outline from Luke 11.

"Father, hallowed be your name.
Your kingdom come.
Give us each day our daily bread,
and forgive us our sins, for we ourselves forgive everyone who is
indebted to us.
And lead us not into temptation."

I find this shorter version of the outline to be easier to remember than when Jesus first taught it in Matthew

6. My favorite author in college was Cliff. He wrote some awesome Notes. Maybe that's why I prefer this more abbreviated version. Let's break down the five categories of the Followers' Prayer Outline.

#1 "Father, Hallowed Be Your Name"

Every conversation we have is completely dependent on the person with whom we're speaking. Naturally, Jesus taught us to address God as our Father who is holy. To call the Almighty Creator and Sustainer of the cosmos, "our Father," is a mind-boggling privilege. We have the right to call him our Father because he chose to adopt us into his holy family. Our union with Christ makes us sons and daughters through faith, so we also have the high honor to call him "Abba".

"Abba" was the common Aramaic term of endearment a child would call their father. In Jesus' day, the people in Israel spoke mostly in Aramaic, and they wrote in Greek. The term also captures the sense of deep respect for a father. Was there a time when you wrote a card or addressed your dad with deep love, gratitude, and respect? How did you address him? Was it, "Dear Dad,"or something similar? This is the idea with the ancient word "Abba." It carried with it a deep and trusting love along with an unwavering respect and admiration.

Jesus taught his followers to begin prayer by acknowledging the new relationship we have with God. Calling the God of their forefathers "Father" was a radically new concept for a first-century Jew. It would have seemed much too informal to them, at least initially. Jewish believers later became accustomed to calling God

"Father," while we can easily take it for granted. To combat this tendency, reflecting on passages such as Ephesians 1:3-14 can remind you of the high privilege you have been given through Christ to be able to call the God of all creation your Father.

Focusing on the reality of *why* you can call him your Father in the heavens will greatly impact *how* you pray. The phrase, "an attitude of gratitude," is applicable here. We're not only acknowledging that Yahweh is our Father, we are thanking him for who he is and who he has made us to be.

A Sample: "Father, You Are Holy"

Here is a sample that might prove helpful to you or to church family. "God of wonders beyond our galaxy, you are holy. The universe declares your majesty, you are holy! All that is good, right, and true is yours. Thank you, heavenly Father, for showing me who Jesus is and for giving me the faith to believe he suffered, died, and rose to life to reign forever. Thank you that, in him, I have a brand-new life, both on this earth and in the next life, with you. I praise you that you are my Father who loves me with an endless love. I believe nothing in the seen or unseen world can ever separate me from your love. You are an amazing Father, full of love and patience for me and for all who trust in your Son. Thank you, Father, for giving me your grace when I don't even recognize it. Thank you, Father, that all of your promises to me are certain and all of your words are true. Help me now to speak with you in a way that honors you and pleases you and makes you smile."

Imagine how much pleasure your heavenly Father finds in hearing you say things like that. Once you develop the habit of spending time thanking God that you are his son or daughter, thoughts about your high privilege of being part of his family will flow much more easily and naturally. As you think of all he has done and is doing, you will acknowledge his character. Thanking him for who he is and what he is doing will come more naturally as you practice. This is the idea behind *hallowed be your name*. We not only need to address God properly as our Father, we must thank him for the kind of Father he is. Consequently, we want everyone we know and love to also recognize God's holiness.

In His Name

In Jesus' day, to use the phrase "in the name of..." meant to refer to everything about the person. The "name" includes the person's character, their reputation, all they are and all they do. It refers to the totality of their being. So, to conclude a prayer with the phrase "in Jesus' name" means we're asking that everything align with who Jesus is, what he did, all he taught, his current rule and reign, and his second coming. Stating that our Father's *name* is "holy" means we are recognizing everything about God is completely pure and righteous. His whole being and everything about him is holy. He can do no wrong. All he is and does is holy, and there is nothing about him that isn't holy. His holiness means he isn't like us at all. Isn't that good news? You wouldn't want God to be like you, would you?

God's holiness encapsulates all of his other qualities: his love, patience, kindness, goodness, faithfulness, persistence, dependability, and truthfulness. In the prayer outline, Jesus taught to begin praying by acknowledging we are praying to his Father and ours, and that the totality of his entirety is only and always holy.

It may be helpful to picture the scene in Isaiah 6:1-7, when Isaiah was taken up into heaven. He saw the Lord seated on a throne with seraphim circling above him calling out; *"Holy, holy, holy is the LORD of hosts; the whole earth is full of his glory."* Immediately, the prophet was seized with the reality of Yahweh's holiness and his own personal sinfulness. I find it helpful to affirm with the seraphim this majestic declaration of Yahweh. He is before all things and in him all things hold together. Let us be quick to acknowledge that we are beginning to understand how marvelous and full of splendor he actually is. As you remind your soul who God is and what he is like, your problems will begin to diminish and your perspective about life will take on new hope. Concentrating on who is listening to your prayer will impact what you say and what you think. You should be less likely to become sidetracked with competing thoughts. It may help you to think of a favorite story that depicts God's character or picture a scene from nature that declares God's holiness. Find what helps you to remain focused as you pour out your heart to God the Almighty, who loves to listen to your prayers.

#2 "Your Kingdom Come"

Jesus' teaching about prayer in Luke 11 came approximately two years after his sermon on the hill in Matthew 5-7. The Lukan prayer simply states *your kingdom come.* In the earlier teaching, Jesus included the phrase, *your will be done on earth as it is in heaven.* This phrase explains what *your kingdom come* means.

Everything and everyone in heaven is in perfect harmony with the will of God. What we're asking in this first request we make of God is for things and people to align with his will. And this is the most unfamiliar and unused part of the prayer outline - one we must spend much more time grappling with in order to understand it's depth and breadth.

How do things happen in heaven? God is always fully obeyed. The angels and all the saints who have gone before us are all there, in paradise in the presence of the Father and the Son. Everyone basks in the love of God and in the power of the Almighty. There is no sin, no sorrow, no injustice, no pain, no loneliness, no hopelessness, and no disobedience. There is only joy and absolute fulfillment and love in the presence of the Father and the Son. I can only imagine.

Kingdom Alignment

Jesus taught us to ask for our lives to align completely with life in the Kingdom. It is a very sweeping request that ranges from ending all injustice to each follower living in full obedience and unwavering devotion to the Lord. Of course, the prayer also means people everywhere will come to faith in Jesus and become sons and daughters of Yahweh. As the Kingdom comes into our lives, homes, businesses, and communities, everything will change. Nothing can remain the same. Just as Jesus taught in Matthew 6, it's about everything happening on earth like it does in heaven, God's way.

Jesus summed up what the kingdom of heaven does when it comes into a life: "*You shall love the Lord your God with all your heart and with all your soul and with all your strength and with all your mind, and your neighbor as yourself.*" Well, that's easy, right?

No! That kind of transformed life only happens as we engage with our Father by asking him to make those changes happen within us. Instead of only asking for our tangible needs, we are to learn how to *first* and *foremost* long for our hearts and minds to be transformed so that we think and act more and more like Jesus. As leaders, we should be longing for those we influence to surrender their lives completely to Jesus and follow his words and ways.

Because asking for the Kingdom to come is so foreign to our human nature, so challenging to maintain, and so misunderstood and underutilized, I will take the rest of this book to demonstrate from the Bible exactly what "Kingdom Come Praying" involves. This is the kind of praying we must learn, especially as leaders of his people, because it does not come to us naturally. It comes super-naturally or a better term is: "Spirit-naturally". To live our lives as Kingdom People and to be a Kingdom Leader, we must be radically dependent on the Spirit of Christ to work in and through us. The *potential* for each of us, and everyone we lead, to become like Jesus is astounding. This is God's will for you and for every Christ-follower you lead, to *participate in the divine nature* (2 Peter 1:4). That is why the remaining four chapters of this book are dedicated to envisioning what "Kingdom Come Praying" can accomplish through your leadership. As a Kingdom leader, the impact you have on others will increase exponentially as you begin to ask, in very specific and strategic ways, for the Kingdom to come in those you lead.

Don't miss the order of Jesus' outline for our praying. It begins with acknowledging who God is and what he is like. He then tells us to talk to our Father about the most important aspect of our lives, Kingdom alignment, which is spiritual transformation and mind renewal that comes through the indwelling Spirit of God. And that is a life-long process.

#3 "Give Us Each Day Our Daily Bread"

The next category is, *Give us each day our daily bread*. The Greek phrase could also be translated, *Give us our bread for tomorrow*. Jesus gave us the freedom to ask our Father for the things we need in life. For his audience, food was the most pressing need. But that's not true for most of us. Thankfully, the request is not limited to food alone but includes everything we need in life.

Tangible needs abound. Sometimes those needs are so heavy we can barely function. Whether these needs involve health, work, finances, relationships (or the lack thereof), legal matters, or an emotional crisis, you and everyone you lead have pressing needs. Have you noticed it is those tangible needs that usually dominate prayer? When prayers are offered in churches or small groups, what kinds of things are typically requested? Isn't it almost always about the tangible things people need – health, safety, jobs, or money?

The reality that our default focus is on physical needs is exactly why Jesus instructed us to pray about Kingdom things *before* we pray about our physical and relational needs. The order of the outline is critically important if we're going to develop our conversations with the Father to the depth he desires. Jesus' brilliance is on magnificent display here, in the *order* of our requests. As you pray first for spiritual transformation, God's kingdom to come, it will greatly impact your perspective on tangible needs. As you ask for the kingdom to come first, it will have a profound impact on how you see physical needs. Therefore, practice asking for spiritual needs first, just like Jesus instructed! That's his plan for us. He knows if we focus on the Kingdom stuff first, which is spiritual transformation, our perspective of tangible needs will change.

Praying for someone's health takes on an entirely new perspective when you begin praying for God to give them his Spirit, flooding their heart with the light of his Word and strengthening them to be able to endure the illness with the joy of the Lord.

The wonderful news is Jesus did include this category of physical needs in The Followers' Prayer Outline. He cares deeply about us, more than we'll ever realize on this side of eternity (Matthew 6:25-34). He knows from his own experience of living as a human how important food, shelter, and clothing are. Just remember they are not the most important aspects of your life. "Kingdom Come Praying" is to be your first and foremost request, which is why chapters three through six of this book are devoted to exploring Paul's prayers.

#4 "And Forgive Us Our Sins"

For most of us, acknowledging our failures to our Father is a part of prayer that's often neglected. Jesus stressed it is critically important for us to keep very short accounts with our Father.

The power of confessing your sins to God can't be overemphasized. Can you remember when you were a child and had to confess your guilt to your parents? Can you remember how you felt before you confessed? Do you remember how the guilt made you feel terrible? Confessing you were the one responsible set you free to experience the discipline you knew you deserved. You didn't want the spanking or being imprisoned in your room, but it was worth it just to be free from the guilt.

We need to confess *all* of our sins *specifically* in order to gain victory over them. You can't begin to conquer a short temper until you acknowledge that you *have* a short temper. Jealousy will continue to dog church members until they begin to confess to the Father every time they feel jealous. That's just the way life works in the Kingdom.

Confessing is the reality of looking within your heart and acknowledging the truth about how you act and feel. It's the act of coming clean with God and accepting the ugliness in you he wants to help you overcome. So, ask yourself a soul-penetrating question: Why don't I confess my sins to God more frequently and more specifically?

Jesus added this part to our prayer outline because he knows how beneficial it will be for every one of his followers. He also knows a powerful way to minimize pride and over-confidence in ourselves is to regularly tell the Father how we've messed up. And don't ever forget that we need to confess both kinds of sin – omission and commission. We usually know when we've done wrong. Those are sins of commission. Equally sinful to God are the times when we fail to do what's right. We fail to love, forgive, encourage, or serve someone in the realm of our influence. Those are sins of omission. It's critically important to confess both types of crimes against God.

Be Specific

The temptation in this area of confession is to use a wide brush stroke and generalize our failures. "God, forgive me for coveting." Do you think that's what your heavenly Father wants to hear? Will that really help you to get serious about dealing with a covetous attitude? Did your mother want to hear, "Mom, sorry for disobeying you"? Or did she want to hear you say, "Please forgive me for not cleaning up my room like you asked me to." You get the point.

Our temptation is to become slack, lazy, or just too busy. We don't really want to think about all of our failures, so we tend to not bring them up when we're praying. Jesus is reminding us we must take the time to keep short accounts with our Father who knows all our secrets. Isn't it ridiculous that we even pretend to keep anything from him?

Who Owes You?

The most powerful reality of confessing sins regularly to God is how it will change our perspective towards others. The sins committed against *you* will diminish the more you honestly acknowledge *your* sins against God. Stop and underline that sentence. Read it a few more times and let that truth sink in. It is true. As you look within and acknowledge all of your sins against the Father, your perspective will be changed.

Think of someone who has wronged you. What did they do or not do? How did it make you feel? Are you having trouble forgiving them, either in your heart or to them personally? Now ask yourself how many times you've committed a similar sin against God. You simply have no reason why you can't forgive the other person's sin against you. None!

Jesus was obviously very intentional with his words. He told us to confess our sins, using the normal word for sins, *hamartia*. It literally means to miss the mark and is the typical word used for all sins against God. Did you catch the word Jesus used to describe when we forgive others? Debts. Jesus taught us to pray and ask the Father to forgive our sins in the same way we forgive everyone *"who is indebted to us."* The word "indebted" means to owe money, unless it's used as a metaphor, like Jesus used it here.

Who owes you something? I can think of lots of people who owe me an apology, some owe me a response (email, text, or call), others owe me more respect, and still others owe me their gratitude. What do people owe you? How big is their indebtedness? These debts are real and hurtful. People really do owe us. But are we entitled to collect, ever?

Seven Times?

Peter asked Jesus how often he should forgive his brother who sinned against him. The standard answer in those days was seven times. Once you hit seven, the person had exhausted their grace allotment and was no longer eligible to be forgiven – so they thought and taught. But Jesus answered Peter by blowing his mind, telling him he should forgive his brother seventy times seven or literally, "*seventy-sevens*". Jesus didn't mean Peter needed to keep count until he reached 490. He overwhelmingly exaggerated the common teaching of the day. His point was forgiveness is without limits. Then he told one of the most profound parables that you'll ever read. Take a few minutes to explore Matthew 18:23-35. Make sure you do the math to compare the two different values of indebtedness.

Realize the people you must forgive probably don't deserve it. In Jesus' story, neither servant deserved forgiveness, and neither do *you*. We can only forgive others on the basis of God's forgiveness. You give someone mercy because God always gives you mercy. Your forgiveness isn't even about your relationship with the other person. It's all about your relationship with God. Forgive them because Jesus wants you to forgive them. Wipe away their small debt to you because your colossal debt to God has been eradicated by Christ. Forgiveness gives your Father in the heavens great pleasure. He is proud of you when you forgive others. It gives him great joy! Focus on that reality when you're struggling to forgive someone who owes you.

#5 "And Lead Us Not Into Temptation"

We're now at the fifth and final category of the Follower's Prayer Outline. Jesus gave us the directive to ask his Father to lead us out of every temptation. The language is a little confusing for us. The way Jesus phrased it makes it sound as if God might very well lead us into temptations. Did this last part of the prayer confuse you when you first memorized it? Do you remember hearing the prayer recited in church, not knowing how this "leading" worked? We must understand exactly what Jesus meant by this last request.

James, one of Jesus' half-brothers, helps us to understand what we already sense in our hearts – that God doesn't tempt us to sin. *Blessed is the man who remains steadfast under trial, for when he has stood the test he will receive the crown of life, which God has promised to those who love him. Let no one say when he is tempted, "I am being tempted by God," for God cannot be tempted with evil, and he himself tempts no one. But each person is tempted when he is lured and enticed by his own desire. Then desire when it has conceived gives birth to sin, and sin when it is fully grown brings forth death* (James 1:12-15).

The Source of Temptations

Where do temptations come from? Temptations to sin are all around us, in society. They come from the "Me Monster" within us and from Satan and his evil domain. Jesus gave us a rhetorical statement that carries great force when we understand correctly how to navigate successfully the countless landmines of temptations.

We understand the origins of temptations and how to overcome them from a classic passage in 1 Corinthians 10:1-13. Many followers of Jesus have memorized v13 (next page). In this passage, the Apostle Paul reminds us God preserved the Hebrew scriptures, the Old Testament, in order to give us instruction, to reveal his ways, and to give us examples of how to live and not live. His point in the first twelve verses is we must be very careful with our lives and do all we can to follow closely after God and avoid sinning as much as possible. Sin always has consequences. Sometimes those consequences are catastrophic, sometimes they are not so great. But all sin is rebellion against God, and it always comes with a cost, some type of consequence. So, not choosing to sin is always your best choice. But we all fail at times. How can we improve?

Here is that powerful verse; *No temptation has overtaken you that is not common to man. God is faithful, and he will not let you be tempted beyond your ability, but with the temptation he will also provide a way of escape, that you may be able to endure it.* What an encouraging truth. We don't have to sin! Your church members don't have to succumb to their internal or external temptations.

How can God keep us from being tempted beyond our ability, as well as give us a way of escape, if he is not present with us? That is at the core of this truth. God *is* with us. The Psalmist wrote: *God is our refuge and strength, a very present help in trouble* (Psalm 46:1). Jesus promised to everyone who trusts in him he would never leave them, forget about them, or abandon them. The Father and the Son are actually present with us every moment of every day through the Spirit who lives within us.

You face all kinds of temptations to sin. Anger, pride, lack of love, coveting, jealousy, bickering, unforgiveness and sexual immorality are all common temptations. Every person you lead faces the same enticements. That's what the Bible reminds us. We all face the same kinds of temptations. They are common to everyone, but we need not give in to all or any of those temptations because God is always faithful to us. He knows what we can handle and what we can't. He is well aware of your strengths and all of your weaknesses. He will challenge you to grow in your dependence on him, but he does not want you to fail him. He wants you to overcome every temptation and he always provides a way of escaping each temptation. And he will test you to help you learn to rely on him.

God Knows Your Limits

Isn't it comforting to know your Father has such intimate knowledge of you that he knows where you're vulnerable? He knows your limits. Your Father knows when you get angry in traffic, are tempted to view porn or feel jealousy towards your co-worker. God's plan for your life is for you to lean on him at all times, especially when you are being tempted. In the next chapters, we will discover much more about *the way of escape* he provides. But for now, be assured you can overcome any temptation by turning to him for help.

This is why Jesus ended our prayer outline by having us ask God to show us the way of escape throughout each day. To do that, we must learn how to live in the *conscious awareness* he is with us. God is your refuge and he is your strength. He is most definitely present in your life, when times are great, when times are tempting, and every time in between.

The outline guides you to end your time of prayer by affirming God is always with you and you need his help. The best discipline you can learn is to live in the constant awareness of God's presence. Develop the habit of thinking about God throughout the day. Take control of your thinking to remind yourself you live every moment under his watchful eye. Realize you don't ever do anything with another person one on one. A third person is ever present, the Spirit of Jesus.

Using the Outline

Jesus' outline is how he tells us to pray. This doesn't mean you can't pray other ways, or you can't begin in the middle of this prayer outline as the need arises. If you have just sinned, then jump right into confessing the sin and then checking your heart to determine if you have forgiven everyone who owes you. Realize this outline is a powerful weapon Jesus gave us to use when we carve out strategic time to talk with our heavenly Father and when we need to flare a quick Kingdom Come Prayer for help.

Commit this outline to memory. Write it in your own words, if that helps you. Keep it taped on your sun visor or to your mirror or laptop screen. Do whatever you need to do to commit this outline of prayer to memory so that you can enjoy the fullness of the abundant life that Jesus came to give us. Use this outline as you intercede for your church.

Jesus' Profound Promise

Before we move on to exploring the four Kingdom Come Prayers in the coming chapters, understanding Jesus' promise about prayer is absolutely essential. On that holy Thursday night, before the cross, Jesus made an astounding promise about prayers being answered. It comes to us from the old Apostle John.

When you read any of John's writings, it is very helpful to understand his context. The Lord did not inspire John to write Scripture until he was a very old man, likely in his 90's. All the other Apostles had long since gone home to live with the Lord in paradise by the time John wrote. No doubt, John read, and probably re-read many times, the New Testament letters written by Matthew, Mark, Luke, Paul, and Peter. Those writings were all completed in the mid to late 60's AD.

Even though he wasn't inspired by the Spirit to write Scripture until very late in his life, he no doubt taught these stories over and over. He had been sharing these unique stories for more than 60 years when, in his twilight years, the Spirit inspired John to write them down. That is why his gospel account is so unique.

Instead of writing what paralleled the other three gospel letters, John recorded several very personal interactions Jesus had with people, along with in depth teachings that help us understand the Kingdom even more. Remember, John personally experienced everything he wrote about. It is the old Apostle John who gave us Jesus' final teaching on that holy Thursday night. It was so profound, he dedicated almost 20 precent of his gospel account to what Jesus did and taught on the evening before the cross. We find it in John 13-17.

When you read John's writings, picture yourself having coffee with the kindest, dearest, most righteous, elderly man you've ever met. Watch his old eyes sparkle with excitement and listen to the passion in his voice as he shares what his beloved Master said and did.

Through John, we hear Jesus make this astonishing promise. As you read his words, underline what stands out to you about prayer.

14:13-14 "Whatever you ask in my name, this I will do, that the Father may be glorified in the Son. If you ask me anything in my name, I will do it."

15:7-8 "If you abide in me, and my words abide in you, ask whatever you wish, and it will be done for you. By this my Father is glorified, that you bear much fruit and so prove to be my disciples."

15:16 "You did not choose me, but I chose you and appointed you that you should go and bear fruit and that your fruit should abide, so that whatever you ask the Father in my name, he may give it to you."

16:23b "Truly, truly, I say to you, whatever you ask of the Father in my name, he will give it to you."

"In My Name"

The obvious question is what does it mean to ask the Father for something in the name of Jesus? You've likely heard lots of people end prayers declaring "in Jesus' name." Is that what he meant for us to say? Do we simply tag on those three words to any request and "presto bingo," we have it? Of course not. That's ridiculous.

Read through Jesus' promise again. He stated it four different ways. The second time he made the promise, in John 15:7-8, he explicitly defined what *"in my name"* means. As Jesus' words remain in us, we are, then and only then, able to ask according to what aligns with his perfect will. As we remain dedicated followers who strive to obey all of his instructions, his words guide our requests. Obedience to Jesus' commands is how you love him and loving him requires prayer. As you pray according to the Bible, you will be asking for his kingdom to come in your church family. That is Jesus' desire. That is what the Father wants to happen in the lives of everyone you lead.

The key to confident asking is praying according to the very words of Jesus. When you pray according to his words, the Father will do whatever you ask. How is that possible? Well, when you pray according to his words, you are praying in Jesus' name, which is in complete alignment with his will. You will be praying the same kinds of prayers Jesus prayed, for the Kingdom to come in the lives of people. Since everything in the Bible was inspired by Jesus' Spirit, the entire Bible is Jesus' words. Jesus himself is the Word of God.

John likely wrote his three short letters after writing his gospel account. In his first letter, 1 John, you hear the apostle echoing Jesus' words from that holy Thursday night. *This is the confidence we have toward him, that if we ask anything according to his will he hears us. And if we know that he hears us in whatever we ask, we know that we have the requests that we have asked of him* (1 John 5:14-15). Remember, he had been experiencing the reality of this promise for more than 60 years when he wrote this letter.

God's will is in black and white. It's written down for us to read over and over again. He has graciously preserved his Scriptures for us down through the centuries. The Follower's Prayer Outline is our God-given guide to praying according to his will. "But I want specifics about his will!", you might be thinking. So do I. The specific answers you need will come through the Spirit as you pray according to this outline given to us by the Son of God, as you keep Jesus' words in you.

Proper Alignment

As your requests align with God's will, you can have complete confidence he will do what you've asked. How do you know his will? That's the ten-million-dollar question, isn't it? You, like me, want to know God's will for your life in all kinds of situations and circumstances. You want specifics. Should I take this job? Should we move? Should I date this person? On and on our questions go, wondering what God's will for us truly is.

That's where the Kingdom Come Prayers come in. They are his will, his very words. In these next four chapters, you will learn specific requests and results as you use the very words of Jesus given through the Apostle Paul.

Use the Follower's Prayer Outline to guide you as you pray for yourself, your family, and everyone you lead. Remember, praying through the outline as Jesus gave it is essential. You can do that in a few minutes, or it can take much longer. However, you don't always have time to pray through the entire outline. That's why it's important to understand the flow, so you can jump in where needed. The next four chapters will guide you how to strategically ask for the Kingdom to come into the lives of those you lead. But you should also make it a practice to give God praises throughout your day. Thank him each time you experience his grace. Confess your failure to him the moment you realize it. Ask for tangible needs as you learn of them. Own the outline Jesus gave you!

Consider tearing page 42 out of this book, to help you put the outline into practice.

The Followers' Prayer Outline – Luke 11:2-4

#1 **Our Father** - Thank your holy, heavenly Father

#2 **Your Kingdom** - Ask for his kingdom to come

#3 **Our Needs** - Ask for tangible needs to be met

#4 **Confess & Forgive** - Confess specific sins and forgive everyone of everything they owe you

#5 **Your Power** - Acknowledge his powerful presence to resist temptations

CHAPTER 3 – ASK FOR THE SPIRIT

Jesus is the King of his kingdom and you are an appointed leader. Whether you're a pastor, bishop, minister, elder, deacon, or director, you have been given a unique role and profound responsibilities. But what is to take priority in your very full schedule? What will you eliminate, not rearrange, so that your priorities resemble those of the Apostle Paul and his team members?

The key to Kingdom leadership is prayer. So, the million-dollar question is: How do Kingdom leaders pray? They pray using the very words of the King. Kingdom Come Prayers have been given to us by the King's Spirit as he inspired the Apostle Paul. You are about to discover how to acquire Jesus' profound promise that his Father will answer *all* of your requests. No, this is not some new "name it and claim it" approach. This type of requesting is purely biblical, taken directly from the pages of Scripture. As your requests align with Jesus himself, which is what it means to ask in his name, the Father will enthusiastically answer in order to make his kingdom come.

The first Kingdom Come Prayer we'll explore is found in Ephesians 1:16-19.

I do not cease to give thanks for you, remembering you in my prayers, that the God of our Lord Jesus Christ, the Father of glory, may give you the Spirit of wisdom and of revelation in the knowledge of him, having the eyes of your hearts enlightened, that you may know what is the hope to which he has called you, what are the riches of his glorious inheritance in the saints, and what is the immeasurable greatness of his power toward us who believe, according to the working of his great might that he worked in Christ when he raised him from the dead and seated him at his right hand in the heavenly places, far above all rule and authority and power and dominion, and above every name that is named, not only in this age but also in the one to come. And he put all things under his feet and gave him as head over all things to the church, which is his body, the fullness of him who fills all in all.

Take a moment to read this prayer again. Underline the one request and the three resulting outcomes we can "know." It's one of the most majestic prayers in the Bible. That's because it comes out of one of the most amazing passages in the Bible, Paul's opening verses of his letter to the believers of the church in the ancient city of Ephesus. If you have a Bible handy, read through vs1-23 of Ephesians before you continue reading the rest of this chapter. Getting the full context of the prayer will definitely help in understanding it more fully and using it more dutifully.

Letters to Gathered Believers

Whenever you read one of the letters to the churches, you'll want to do so as if you are reading it with all of the members of your own church. These letters, called the Epistles, were first and foremost written to churches, to all the believers in those cities, as they gathered together to worship and learn. We tend to read these portions of Scripture as a personal letter from God, and that they are, only secondly. They are, first and foremost, letters to the gathered believers and thus we need to understand them in that context, as if we are all reading it together and considering the implications for us as Jesus' local church. This proper understanding of the letters makes an enormous difference in how we understand and apply the truths therein.

It is helpful to remember, too, each word written comes from the inspiration of the Holy Spirit. This portion of Ephesians is exceptionally majestic and grandiose in describing how God has poured out his grace on us. It is surprising the Spirit refers to Jesus as God's "mystery." The specific words the Spirit inspired Paul to write were very intentional, as of course is true in all of the Bible. It is important we think about the exact words and strive to understand them. It is also freeing to admit that, at times, the words can be very intimidating and difficult to grasp. The prayer itself has a majesty and richness all its own. That is why we must explore it fully in order to be able to own it personally.

One Primary Request

Over the years, theologians and scholars have grown in their understanding of the original Greek language. So much more is known about it now than even 100 years ago. Thousands of manuscripts have been discovered in recent decades. The original texts obviously no longer exist. However, we have an overabundance of copies for complete certainty as to exact wording in the originals. Most New Testament translations we have today typically come from the same Greek translation, which is a compilation of thousands of ancient manuscripts. However, English translators choose different words and phrases to try to capture the original meaning of the Greek and Aramaic (the spoken language of Jesus' day). Because our English language is constantly evolving, new Bible translations are continually being produced. Some translations focus on finding the closest "word-for-word" meaning, while others emphasize a "thought-for-thought" philosophy. I have chosen the English Standard Version (ESV) for most passages due to its "essentially literal" translation style.

Depending on the translation you use, it is sometimes difficult to tell if this prayer in Ephesians has one request or multiple requests. The most reputable scholars today agree this Kingdom Come Prayer is actually one request with three incredible results.

THE REQUEST - He Gives His Spirit

The request is this: *that the God of our Lord Jesus Christ, the Father of glory, may give you the Spirit of wisdom and of revelation in the knowledge of him.* Paul was led by the Spirit to intercede continually for the believers in each of the new churches. This is what a Kingdom leader does. It is clear Paul and his team continually and faithfully prayed for the churches. They knew these followers desperately needed God's help through his Spirit to be able to remain true to Christ. His primary request was that the Father would give them his Spirit so they could know God better and better. God wanted those believers to continually increase in their understanding of his Word and his ways, and he wants the same for you and me and for everyone we influence. God's desire is for his people to know him better and better so they will trust him more faithfully and love him with a deeper devotion. If you think about it, it makes perfect sense.

Of course, our Creator and Savior wants us to know him better and better. He wants us to understand him, as much as we possibly can. He wants us to know he is completely trustworthy and he is always working for what is best for us and his kingdom. He wants us to believe every word he has given us in the Bible came from him, and it is all unequivocally true. Your heavenly Father wants you to develop a deep desire to *want* those you lead to know him so well *they* will learn to ask him for his help. God's will is that everyone in your circle of influence comes to understand the Bible so they can apply it in every situation they face (Philippians 2:12-13). You will help them develop as you faithfully ask God to give them *the Spirit of wisdom and of revelation in the knowledge of him.*

Full Knowledge

In this Kingdom Come Prayer, the word for "knowledge" the Spirit led Paul to use is a special word. It's a compound word that adds a prefix to the customary word for knowledge. It's not just wisdom, but full, complete, and precise understanding. The prefix helps to convey how God wants us to have a very personal and intimate understanding of who he is and what he is like. You have many acquaintances, but you probably only have a few close friends you know really well. What if you knew God as well as you know your closest friend?

Jesus used this compound word when he described how he and the Father know each other. *"All things have been handed over to me by my Father, and no one knows the Son except the Father, and no one knows the Father except the Son and anyone to whom the Son chooses to reveal him."* (Matthew 11:27) The Father and the Son have this complete and intimate knowledge of each other. They know each other so well they are always in harmony, in total unity in their actions and desires. The Father wants his people to get to know him in a similar way as his Son knows him.

He Chose Us

The request in this Kingdom Come Prayer is to ask the Father to help us know him better and better. But how does that actually happen? You read above what Jesus emphatically stated: only those to whom he chooses to reveal the Father will ever know him as their Father. That is an amazing truth, but it can be confusing too.

Did you know the only reason you believe in Jesus and can understand the Bible is because Jesus himself chose to reveal it to you? In the opening paragraphs of his letter, Paul reminded the believers in the church in Ephesus that God chose them before he even created the world. He adopted them into his family, forgave all their sins, purchased them out of slavery to self and

Satan, and lavished his grace on them. Of course, the exact same is true for you, me, and everyone you lead. Jesus made known to us the mystery of his Father's will – that all who believe in the Son for the forgiveness of their sins are rescued from the curse of death and hell. I recommend you pause now and re-read Ephesians 1:3-14 as well as 2:1-10 so that you can soak in the spiritual blessings that are yours in Christ.

The takeaway is the only good coming out of us is because of the good God continues to put within us. It is God's grace that enables you to do what is right and reject what is wrong. He is the one working in and through us to bring his light into the lives of those we interact with each day.

Jesus said he reveals his Father to his people. He makes known to us who his Father is and what is really true in this life and the one to come. Through the Holy Spirit, the Father gives us enlightenment and understanding. The Greek verb translated "reveal" is *apokalypto*. As a noun, it's typically translated "revelation." "Apocalypse" is a direct transliteration from this Greek word. To Jesus' audience, when they heard the word apocalypse, they pictured something coming to light that was previously hidden or not understood. The last book of the Bible is The Revelation of Jesus Christ. Apocalypse isn't about aliens invading earth or giant meteors barreling toward us, it's the unveiling of God's truth to his people. God even tells us the only way people can understand the Bible is if he gives them the ability to understand it. Otherwise, people's minds are veiled to its truths. On their own, without his help, they can't comprehend it's meaning (2 Corinthians 4:1-6). This is how you can pray for the saints *and* the sinners you lead, so they will be filled with the Spirit so their heart's eyes will be flooded with the Father's truth, whatever truth they currently need.

Through the Spirit

Back to the prayer request. We are to ask the Father to give his Spirit, who has all wisdom and revelation. It's not only how we all came to know and believe in Jesus initially, and it is the only way we can continue to grow closer to him. The Spirit of God gives us understanding as he opens our mind and heart to the truths we read in the Bible or hear in a sermon, podcast, or song. That is what God wants you to ask him to do in you and in your church family! His will is to give all the wisdom and insight needed to enable his children to follow him with an undivided heart. His will is that we all grow to maturity.

The only way to understand God is through the Spirit's help. Do we need more of the Spirit? Yes and no. When someone receives Jesus as Lord and Savior, they are regenerated, or born from above. The phrase is also translated "born again." The Spirit of God renews their heart and regenerates their spirit so they are a new creation in Christ. Their identity is now in Christ Jesus because they have been adopted into his family. The Father gave them to his Son as a cherished gift. These statements are all synonymous ways the Bible describes the miracle of a person being forgiven of all their sins. In his conversation with Nic one night, Jesus described this new birth (John 3:1-21) and John stated we were *born of God* in 1 John 3:9.

Doesn't the prayer request make even more sense now? God made you his own so you could know him intimately and have a vibrant and dependent relationship with your heavenly Father. Instead of as in human relationships where the older we become the more we grow independent from our parents, in Christ we grow more and more dependent on our Father the longer we live.

So, does the Spirit come and go? Is that why we are to ask the Father to give us his Spirit? No. The Spirit doesn't leak out of us, but our faith certainly does. Our commitment to Christ and our love for the Father definitely wains. Therefore, we need to be constantly renewed. The Spirit led Paul to write in Romans 12:2: *Do not be conformed to this world, but be transformed by the renewal of your mind, that by testing you may discern what is the will of God, what is good and acceptable and perfect.* The first Kingdom Come Prayer request is how someone is transformed by the renewing of their minds. And we all need a ton of mind renewal! God knows this better than we do, so he gives us his Spirit in order to renew and transform how we think about life, Jesus, and his kingdom. He is in the business of giving his people his Son's values and perspectives on life. We can only receive and maintain a right perspective through the Spirit's ongoing assistance as he shines his truth into the dark and confused places of our hearts and minds.

It's All About Light

What existed before God created light? The Bible opens with: *In the beginning, God created the heavens and the earth. The earth was without form and void, and darkness was*

51

over the face of the deep. And the Spirit of God was hovering over the face of the waters.

And God said, "Let there be light," and there was light (Genesis 1:1-3).

Light seems to be one of God's favorite metaphors. Why? Because he created it. He is the one who imagined light and chose to make it become a reality. What a perfect metaphor it is! It is tangible and relatable so every language group and all peoples throughout history have known the difference between dark and light. Dark hides what is true and real.

So how does God give us his Spirit of wisdom and revelation so that we can know him better? He shines the light of his truth into the dark places of our hearts and minds to make us see him. Without light you can't see. Without the Spirit bringing light to God's Word and our lives, we can't see to know God's will and what we should do or not do.

Consider 2 Corinthians 4:3-6: *And even if our gospel is veiled, it is veiled to those who are perishing. In their case the god of this world has blinded the minds of the unbelievers, to keep them from seeing the light of the gospel of the glory of Christ, who is the image of God. For what we proclaim is not ourselves, but Jesus Christ as Lord, with ourselves as your servants for Jesus' sake. For God, who said, "Let light shine out of darkness," has shone in our hearts to give the light of the knowledge of the glory of God in the face of Jesus Christ.*

Think about this truth for a minute. God chose to shine in you the light of the knowledge of his glory, which is his Son, Jesus Christ. That means he unveiled your dark mind to be able to understand and accept the truth of who Jesus is and what he offers to all who will receive him. I don't want to take the word for "knowledge" differentiation too far, but it is really interesting how the Spirit led Paul to use the normal word for knowledge here rather than the word for full and intimate knowledge. God shines into our hearts the general knowledge and understanding of who Jesus is. From this point on in our lives, he wants to give us more intimate knowledge of himself, his Son, and his Spirit.

Our Heart's Eyes

The Kingdom Come Prayer request in Ephesians 1:18 identifies exactly how the Father will help his people to know him more fully: *having the eyes of your hearts enlightened, that you may know…* The heart is where all of our emotions and our desires live. This phrase of clarification was included in the prayer request so we would know what needs to happen in our most inward part.

What are the eyes of our hearts? It is a vivid metaphor of how our emotions and our deep-seated desires can be wrongly influenced, darkened by our sinful nature. The only way to see what is right and what is wrong is if God shines his light into our darkness. The eyes of the human heart are blinded and can only be given sight by God's gracious miracle. The Lord is illustrating how our innermost being needs to be fully enlightened to the words and ways of God. That is precisely why we are to ask our Father to give his Spirit, who has all wisdom and revelation, to bring clarifying light to the heart's eyes of everyone in your church. We can also think of it as God's Spirit gives us corrective lenses with a new prescription yielding HD, 20/20 vision.

But it's not like those you lead have 62 percent of the Spirit in them and they need to increase to 85 percent. Every true believer has 100% of the Spirit living within. The critical question is: Does he have 100% of them? No, of course not! None of us are there. As long as we live on this sin-saturated earth, we'll never give ourselves fully to the Spirit, every waking moment. Thankfully, progress is definitely God's will for us. He wants us to desire to give ourselves fully to his Spirit so we will have maximum Kingdom influence. We're all on the same journey of growing into the kind of people who are increasingly influenced by the Spirit of God. What you and I need more than anything else is to be more influenced by the Spirit of God throughout every moment of every day, so we can then influence others and intercede for them.

Spirit Filled

The Epistles, the fancy name for the letters to the churches in the New Testament, are almost exclusively about teaching Jesus' followers how to follow him with absolute devotion. They interpret and apply Jesus' teachings for us with illustrations such as: *And do not get drunk with wine, for that is debauchery, but be filled with the Spirit, addressing one another in psalms and hymns and spiritual songs, singing and making melody to the Lord with your heart, giving thanks always and for everything to God the Father in the name of our Lord Jesus Christ, submitting to one another out of reverence for Christ* (Ephesians 5:18-21).

Most of us know what it's like to be drunk. I'll spare you from going into a lot of personal testimony about my knowledge of intoxication. When you're drunk, you are not in control of yourself. You say and do things that you would never say and do otherwise. It's a very appropriate analogy. Instead of being under the influence of alcohol, weed, or drugs, God tells us to live under the growing influence of the Spirit of Jesus. As you ask the Father to give you more and more of his Spirit's influence, you'll become the kind of leader described in this passage. You will live in thankfulness to God for everything good in your life, for giving you the opportunity to influence others by serving them, praying for them, and putting them ahead of yourself, because you are in awe of Jesus. When you truly put others ahead of yourself, it is because you are under the influence of the Spirit. Paul and his team constantly prayed for other believers because they were led by the Spirit to do so. Being under his control is also described in the Bible as being filled with the Spirit or being led by the Spirit. They are synonymous. Your goal in life is to live each day with the Spirit's help. *But I say, walk by the Spirit, and you will not gratify the desires of the flesh…If we live by the Spirit, let us also keep in step with the Spirit* (Galatians 5:16 & 25).

The more the Spirit of God influences believers, the more they will experience the impact, the fruit of his influence: *But the fruit of the Spirit is love, joy, peace, patience, kindness, goodness, faithfulness, gentleness, self-control; against such things there is no law. And those who belong to Christ Jesus have crucified the flesh with its passions and desires* (Galatians 5:22-24).

Only the Spirit can persuade you to love others more than you love yourself. When you put the interests of others ahead of your own and pray regularly for them, it is because you are being led by the Spirit of Christ. When you are genuinely patient and kind to an irate church member, it's because of the Spirit's influence in you. People are patient and kind every day without the help of the Spirit of God, but their motive isn't *from* God. They are likely doing it for what they might get out of that action, how it will benefit them or their reputation. But when you're drunk on the Spirit, he will lead you to be faithful to God. He will empower you to have self-control in the face of that besetting temptation that often takes you down. He will inspire you to pray for your church family with an unwavering diligence. Remember Epaphras (pg. 8)?

Here's how you can word this prayer request for those you influence: "I ask you, my glorious Father of my Lord Jesus Christ, to give them your Spirit, who has all wisdom and revelation, to help them know you more intimately by enlightening their heart's eyes to know…"

Three Gigantic Results

The rest of the passage reveals what God wants to accomplish through this one prayer request. There are three results, each of which can radically change a person's life: *that you may know* (1) *what is the hope to which he has called you,* (2) *what are the riches of his glorious inheritance in the saints, and* (3) *what is the immeasurable greatness of his power toward us who believe.*

These three results are the byproduct of the Father giving his people his Spirit to know him better, shining the light of his truth into their hearts.

Let's consider the three results one by one. Remember, this type of praying is what Jesus meant when he taught us to pray *"Your kingdom come."* These Kingdom Come Prayers are all cause and effect requests. God teaches us to ask him for something specific so that he can bring about certain changes in our lives in order for us to be better aligned with his kingdom ways.

Kingdom Come Praying is an entirely different way of asking the Father for his help. This kind of praying involves the Spirit working within hearts and minds to bring about righteous change. As we think about what changes are needed, we can then ask for his help accordingly. Therefore, we can approach these prayers from two different angles. We can recognize what is lacking in someone's life and pray the kind of request that will bring about that needed result. Or, we can base our prayers on the specific requests we want to happen. All of this will be much clearer as we work through this and the other Kingdom Come Prayers.

Let's look again at the request and the three results: *that the God of our Lord Jesus Christ, the Father of glory, may give you the Spirit of wisdom and of revelation in the knowledge of him, having the eyes of your hearts enlightened, that you may know what is the hope to which he has called you, what are the riches of his glorious inheritance in the saints, and what is the immeasurable greatness of his power toward us who believe,*

We are asking the Father to give his Spirit so he is known more intimately, in order that these three critical truths are understood with greater assurance. These are the three things God wants us to understand about his kingdom as we get to know him better:

1. What is the hope of *his* calling

2. What are the riches of *his* glorious inheritance

3. What is the immeasurable greatness of *his* power

Read through these three results again. To whom do all three belong? It is God's hope, his inheritance, and his power. His people bring nothing to the table. The only thing believers can give back to God is their love, loyalty, and devotion. And that's all he requires.

1st Result – His Hope

The Father wants his people to really grasp *what is the hope to which he has called you*. God the Father has called believers into his hope. As the preceding verses in Ephesians 1 declare, God chose to adopt each Christ-follower and forgive all of their sins by punishing his Son in their place. That is the mystery of his will. And he chose to do that with people from every ethnicity and language group.

This is sure and certain hope. We have been rescued from standing before a holy God in self-defense. Self-defense before God will always result in a guilty verdict, which will lead to eternal separation from him. The crimes against God are all the sins people commit, the greatest being the rejection of his grace. The joy of our salvation is that we are judged righteous because of Jesus' righteousness. Because the Father has shown the light of his Truth, the Lord Jesus, into our hearts and we have believed him, we have an absolutely certain hope about our future. Our Father wants each of us to understand this truth with such confidence that it changes our daily perspective about how we see life.

The wonderful news about the certainty of our hope is it has absolutely nothing to do with us. We can't earn it and we definitely don't deserve it. The reason is simple. No one calls themselves to God. No one wakes up one morning and decides to be adopted into his family. God calls. He chooses. Your hope is grounded in his calling. That is why it is a rock-solid certainty. That is why we can know without an ounce of doubt that we live in his invisible presence on this earth and when we leave here, we will live in his visible presence forever. Imagine how the power of this reality might impact your church family if they lived in the consciousness of it every day.

Hope may be the greatest need of the people you lead. Hopelessness abounds in our world. It's heartbreaking to think about the issues teens deal with today compared to my teenage years in the 70's. We've never seen teenage suicide to the extent it's happening today. With political turmoil amidst a pandemic and economic uncertainty, where do people who are far from Christ even begin to find hope?

When Hope is Lacking

But followers of Jesus do have hope. When you sense someone in your church is feeling hopeless, the solution is to cry out to your Father to give them his Spirit so they can know him, having their heart flooded with his light to comprehend the hope of his calling.

When the Bible talks about hope, it isn't an uncertain wish, like "we hope it will all happen as God says." Our hope is certain and without question. Our hope is God's future, one that only he knows, but a future he has chosen to reveal to us.

When he tells us that he wants us to know the hope of his calling, it is because he wants us to not be fearful of the future, or the present. Our loving Father wants us to trust him completely and believe that he is in absolute control, especially when circumstances steal away all hope and joy. We not only have this sure hope that God is with us and he is for us, we also know unequivocally that our eternal future is absolutely secure because it is dependent on what Christ did for us, not on anything we might have done or will do in service to him.

When the New Testament mentions hope, it especially emphasizes the eternal hope of being free from God's judgment. Galatians 5:5 reads: *For through the Spirit, by faith, we ourselves eagerly wait for the hope of righteousness.* This verse is referring to the righteousness that will be ours when Jesus returns, sin is eradicated, and the new earth is created. Our struggle against sin will be forever removed and we will live in the fullness of God's righteous rule and reign in a life of only love, joy and fulfillment. For believers who are currently suffering excruciating trials, they need to know the sure hope of the life that awaits them. The Epistles speak about this hope frequently because those first believers were under constant persecution for their faith in Jesus. For those of us whose lives are less threatening, it's more difficult to have an eternal focus on the life to come because life here is pretty darn good. Your intercession for others will help them enjoy a clearer, eternal focus. Kingdom Come Praying by you for them will help them think more about God and his eternity.

The Hope of His Calling

In Ephesians 4:1 & 4 Paul wrote: *I therefore, a prisoner for the Lord, urge you to walk in a manner worthy of the calling to which you have been called…There is one body and one Spirit – just as you were called to the one hope that belongs to your calling.*

Our hope comes from God's calling. By calling us into his family and making us his very own sons and daughters, we now have a sure hope for the future, and the present. God wants you to keep asking him to give others his Spirit so they will grow closer to him and have increasing confidence in the fact that he chose them and called them to himself. He wants them to feel secure in all that his calling entails.

God has promised he will wipe away all that is evil from this world, dry up every tear, and eradicate all suffering and all injustice. He isn't going to overhaul this broken world. He's promised to create a new world, a new paradise for us to live with him in his visible presence. That is his inheritance he promises to us. What a hope that is!

Of course, it's super difficult to imagine. My view about heaven for a long time was a bunch of winged angel-like people singing hymns non-stop. That didn't sound too much like heaven at all. As a matter of fact, that seemed more like hell to me. Sorry, but as a young adult, that's exactly how I felt about heaven. I had a terribly wrong picture of the new world to come. God wants us to be excited about our forever lives with him in an ageless age. It will be so amazing we cannot begin to comprehend the reality of it. But imagine your very best day, the most excited you've ever been about a time in your life, and then biggie size that with a triple shot and a few 5-Hour Energy drinks. The most beautiful place you've ever visited and the most fulfilled moment you've ever experienced can't begin to compare with your forever life in the stunning new earth in the visible presence of God. If the Grand Canyon, the Swiss Alps, the Caribbean and the Northern Lights are from a broken creation, imagine how the new earth will look! Sin will have no influence on nature.

If you or someone you know is feeling hopeless, you now know what to ask of him. Simply ask, and keep asking, the glorious Father of your Lord Jesus Christ to give them his Spirit of wisdom and revelation so they can know God more personally and thus better understand the hope of his calling on their life. He *has* to answer this request. He *will* do it, just as Jesus promised. But you must ask and keep on asking and seek and keep on seeking and knock and keep on knocking. Your Father wants to give his Holy Spirit's influence and inspiration to everyone called into his kingdom, each person under your watchful care.

2nd Result – His Inheritance

The second result that our Father wants us to comprehend is also in Ephesians 1:18; *what are the riches of his glorious inheritance in the saints.* God wants his people to know him more intimately so they can better comprehend the riches of his glorious inheritance. Hope and inheritance are inseparable. Our hope is his promised inheritance will definitely happen. Our certainty that a celestial prosecuting attorney won't be able to overturn our receiving this inheritance comes from the fact that it is God's promised gift to us.

The wording is a bit surprising. You would think it is *our* inheritance that we receive in the new world. That's how we think about inheriting money or possessions here on earth. If a wealthy family member dies and leaves you money, land, or property, it is *your* inheritance. But God surprises us. He says it is actually *his* inheritance *in the saints*. It's not just his inheritance, it is *the riches of his glorious inheritance* he wants us to know all about and have confidence that it is already ours. Remember, we are God's own possession. He bought us with the price of his Son's life. When the end comes, God will have all of his purchased people with him. Jesus will live forever with every soul the Father has given to him. The Spirit will have every person who has been born from him (John 3:5-8). *We* are God's inheritance! He will inherit the work of his grace over the span of history to have every man, woman, and child he has delivered living with him in his glorious kingdom. He will show us just how truly majestic, loving, and full of splendor he truly is.

Read the description of God's promised inheritance from Revelation 21:1-7 several times and take time to soak it in as you ponder its reality.

Then I saw a new heaven and a new earth, for the first heaven and the first earth had passed away, and the sea no longer existed. I also saw the Holy City, new Jerusalem, coming down out of heaven from God, prepared like a bride adorned for her husband.

Then I heard a loud voice from the throne:

Look! God's dwelling is with humanity,

and He will live with them.

They will be His people,

and God Himself will be with them

and be their God.

Death will no longer exist;

grief, crying, and pain will exist no longer,

because the previous things have passed away.

Then the One seated on the throne said, "Look! I am making everything new." He also said, "Write, because these words are faithful and true." And He said to me, "It is done! I am the Alpha and the Omega, the Beginning and the End. I will give water as a gift to the thirsty from the spring of life. The victor will inherit these things, and I will be his God, and he will be My son."

All of the challenges and hassles and hardships of life on planet earth will be remembered no more. There will be no crime, no wars, no disease, no suicide, no cutting, no immorality, no hatred, no jealousy, no back-stabbing, no loneliness, no gender confusion, no inferiority, no prejudices, no depression, no Covid viruses – only love, joy, peace, patience, kindness, goodness, faithfulness, gentleness, and self-control.

Our Guarantee

"But how do I know for sure this will all happen and that I'll be included?", someone may ask you. We have a guarantee. We have an eternal membership card that can never be lost or made void. We have been forever sealed with this guarantee, and the guarantee is a person. He is the Holy Spirit. He is our certainty.

God's purpose was that we Jews who were the first to trust in Christ would bring praise and glory to God. And now you

Gentiles have also heard the truth, the Good News that God saves you. And when you believed in Christ, he identified you as his own by giving you the Holy Spirit, whom he promised long ago. The Spirit is God's guarantee that he will give us the inheritance he promised and that he has purchased us to be his own people. He did this so we would praise and glorify him (Ephesians 1:12-14, NLT).

The Saints

Let's run down a short rabbit trail. There has been a lot of confusion over the term "saints." Most of the people you lead are probably saints, hopefully all of them are. Saints are not those who live extraordinary lives as God's leaders and after they die, get their own statue. Honoring wonderful role models is great, and we should do that. But to dub someone a saint because they have done extraordinary things is completely wrong, according to the Bible. *Every* person who God has called to be his own is a saint. The same Greek word is translated either "holy" or "saint." It means "set apart" or "other". Every believer in Christ has been set apart by God to be his very possession. God is holy and since we are his in Christ, we too are holy. The way you live does not make you a saint or an un-saint! We are only saints because we belong to Christ Jesus. It is our identity as the children of God.

Also, God's inheritance will be selflessly shared among all his saints. Sharing inheritance doesn't usually work too well in families in our world. Why is that? Easy answer. It's due to the sins of jealousy, coveting, and selfishness – the traits of the "Me Monster." Where none of these sins exist, sharing the inheritance will not only be possible, it will be exactly what each of us will *want* to do! Now that's an exceedingly cool thought.

To solidify our thinking about God's hope and his inheritance, let's turn to the Spirit's inspiration to the apostle Peter. *Praise the God and Father of our Lord Jesus Christ. According to His great mercy, He has given us a new birth into a living hope through the resurrection of Jesus Christ from the dead and into an inheritance that is imperishable, uncorrupted, and unfading, kept in heaven for you. You are being protected by God's power through faith for a salvation ready to be revealed in the last time* (1 Peter 1:3-5, HCSB).

This is the inheritance your Father wants his people to grasp. Knowing all about our future inheritance and believing with confidence in its certainty can greatly impact priorities and how people value life. How do we grow in our understanding of this inheritance? How can the reality of the forever life that's coming drain the dread of what we have to deal with now? Do what God says. Ask him to give his Spirit of wisdom and revelation so everyone who calls your church "home" can get to know God better as he sheds light on their deepest feelings regarding this future inheritance that is kept in heaven for us all. When the cares of this world and all the things that require our time and attention become overwhelming, ask the Father to give his Spirit so others can refocus on what really matters. After all, it's only his people that will be in his new world. Houses, cars, jobs, positions, and 401ks will all be dissolved and replaced with the beautifully eternal things of the Kingdom. Our hope is unwavering because Jesus lives to see it to fruition. He can't wait to share his inheritance with all of us.

3rd Result – His Power

At this point in his praying, the Apostle Paul seems to have been overcome with the splendor of the majesty that is ours in Christ. It's as if there weren't enough words for him to adequately describe the benefits in asking the Father to give us his Spirit. The 3rd result is found in its entirety in 1:19-23: that we will know *what is the immeasurable greatness of his power toward us who believe, according to the working of his great might that he worked in Christ when he raised him from the dead and seated him at his right hand in the heavenly places, far above all rule and authority and power and dominion, and above every name that is named, not only in this age but also in the one to come. And he put all things under his feet and gave him as head over all things to the church, which is his body, the fullness of him who fills all in all.*

Wow! Read it again. Read it one more time. Good granny! What a truth this is. It's so big that the Spirit led Paul to use four different words for power. Circle "power" in the first line of this passage. From that Greek word comes the word "dynamite". Circle "working". The Greek word is "energeian". It's God's energy that is doing the work. Next, circle the word "might." This word is also translated power, dominion, and strength. Lastly, circle "worked." This word is yet another Greek word for ability, force, strength, or might. A very literal translation of the phrase is: *what is the infinite mega power toward us...according to the energy of his great strength that he forced in Christ.* What message is God trying to convey to us?

God doesn't want us to just know his power that is available to us, he wants us to know how immeasurably great his power is. He wants us to understand his power is exceedingly, incomparably, incredibly, and surpassingly great. It's no surprise Greek word for great is "mega." God wants you to know how infinitely mega powerful he is, and his power is ready to be used in lives of everyone in your church family or ministry.

As we grow in our intimate knowledge of our loving, heavenly Father, and trust him more faithfully, we'll also understand more of the magnitude of his limitless power that is ready and waiting to be used on behalf of his people. He tells us it is the very same power the Father exploded when he raised Jesus from the dead and put him in the place of ultimate authority. This lofty passage helps us to better understand it took God's unlimited energy to bring about the resurrection of Jesus. It wasn't that the Father could just snap his fingers and make Jesus alive again. God was conquering sin and death. He overcame Satan and all of his demons. This passage helps us understand the fullness and the magnitude of the power of God that was required to bring the Lamb of God back to life. We should be able to appreciate the resurrection of Jesus better as we ask God to give us his Spirit so that we can more fully comprehend his power.

Believers can be set free from fears of wars, terrorism, pandemics, and political scandals by focusing on the reality of God's power and Jesus' authority. Jesus controls all that happens in the seen world and the unseen world. We don't have to worry about demons or Satan or their influence. When worry or fear attack, ask your loving heavenly Father to give his Spirit of wisdom and revelation so the assurance of his absolute reign will prevail. Jesus rules and reigns over everything and everyone in the spirit realm and in our world too. We need God's help through his Spirit to keep this reality in the forefront of our cerebral matter.

When Hard Times Come

Some have been misled to believe that because of Christ's authority and power, faithful believers will be delivered from persecution and poverty. That is a terrible lie from the pit of hell, and it smells like smoke. Having the fullness of God's incredible power available to you does not mean you won't face hardships, sickness, and financial challenges. It does not mean you will never be made fun of for your faith. Having his power doesn't mean you will not face danger or terminal illness. Let's face it, we all have to die one way or another.

Jesus actually promised his people they would face all kinds of persecution and hardship *because* of their faith in him. Recall from Chapter 1 that Luke wrote in Acts 14 about the countless afflictions believers must face to enter the kingdom of God. On that holy Thursday night, Jesus warned the disciples, and us, trouble in this world is inevitable. That is why we intercede for our fellow followers to be given the Spirit, so they can know the power of God to help them stand strong in the face of every trial.

Jesus' people have been facing persecution, martyrdom, enslavement, and every other hardship in life since his church was birthed in Jerusalem almost 2,000 years ago. Remember, it was John's faithful brother, James, one of the inner three, who was murdered for his faith in Christ (Acts 12:1-2). Before him, one of the first deacons, Stephen, was stoned to death (Acts 7:54-60). Was God not powerful enough to stop either of these murders? We all know that answer, but we can find ourselves really confused at times, especially when very bad things happen to really good people. What makes it even tougher is when a non-believing friend or co-worker asks you why God let such a senseless tragedy happen at all.

God is always restraining evil, the darkness of Satan and his kingdom, and the evil that is part of our selfish human nature. He doesn't want any of the evil to happen, but he has created a world of choice, and it is our choices that open the way for all kinds of evil. There are two kingdoms in this world. There is the dark kingdom of Satan and Jesus' kingdom of light. Everyone and everything is in either one or the other.

Those of us who have been called out of the dark domain and into the Kingdom of light and life are so blessed and privileged. We are protected by God's power to be his people in a dark and dying world. We have his power working within us so we can say "no" to every temptation and "yes" to living in Jesus' rightness. We have God's power so we can overcome everything this world and the Evil One throws at us. We even have the power to be able to give up our life in order to stand in steadfast devotion to Jesus Christ.

God's power to help us is essential to living the abundant life Jesus promised. By abundance, he certainly was not referring to possessions, safety, and health. This abundant life is all about knowing *his* Father as *our* Father and belonging to him as his most treasured possession. The abundant life is Kingdom life which is fueled through Kingdom Come Praying.

How His Power Works

Let's get very practical with how the availability of God's power works in our lives. Let's say a member of your church has an addiction to pornography, or maybe they are dealing with strong feelings toward the same sex, or they're thinking about committing adultery or even suicide. One of the best things you can do, if not the very best, is to intercede for them. Pray this Kingdom Come Prayer for them and keep praying and keep interceding for them until they are overcoming the temptation consistently. You will ask your glorious Father to give them his wise and revealing Spirit to shine in this dark place in their heart so they can experience his power to resist the temptation each time it comes. Pray that the Spirit will show them how God's power is available to them to not only resist the temptation, but also to suppress even the thought of such an act. What they need is the power of God working in their heart and head so *his* energy replaces their weakness to this sin. They need the Spirit to reveal to them just how evil these desires are, bringing light into their dark thinking, so they can know the power of Christ to overcome.

Jesus talked a lot about conquering the darkness that surrounds us in Revelation Chapters 2-3. To each of the seven churches, he gave a captivating promise to everyone who conquers temptations to sin. We can only conquer temptations with the help of the power of God working in our hearts and minds. We must understand our desperate need for God and his Spirit to help us live lives that please him.

We all need God's power. You know you need his power. The believers you lead *need* to know that his power is available to them every time they call out to him. They need to know that God is working in and through them with his power even when it's unclear what he is doing. Your children need to know that God is working when they don't feel like he's doing anything. Your student needs God's power to be able to wait for him to open the right door. Experiencing the power of God comes through asking the Father to give his Spirit of wisdom and revelation, so darkened hearts are flooded with the light of his truth.

Tear out the prayer outline on page 73 and keep it with you as a reminder of how to pray for your people.

Kingdom Come Prayer #1

Ephesians 1:17-19

THE REQUEST

I ask you, the glorious Father of my Lord Jesus Christ, to give those I lead your Spirit who has all wisdom and revelation, to help them know you more fully, having their hearts flooded with your light...

1st Result

so they will know the hope of your calling...

2nd Result

so they will comprehend the riches of your glorious inheritance in the saints...

3rd Result

so they will begin to grasp the greatness of your power that's available to all who believe.

CHAPTER 4 – ASK FOR POWER

The second Kingdom Come Prayer is also from the letter to the Ephesians and is found in 3:16-19. Think for a moment about how the Spirit of God led the Apostle Paul to write this letter. Coming out of the first prayer in Chapter 1, he then explained immeasurable riches of God's grace to his people in forgiving their sins and making them to be his holy nation, members of God's very household.

The truths that Paul articulated so majestically *between* the two prayers are precisely what propels him to share the second prayer. The first prayer, in 1:17-19, is a request for the Father to give us his Spirit, who has all wisdom and revelation, so that we can know him more personally and thus better understand his hope, his inheritance, and his power available to all believers. The verses between the two prayers are packed with rich doctrines that explain what and who we were, what

Christ has done, and the new creation he has made us to be:

† We were dead to God because of our sins

† He saved us when we were in rebellion to him

† He has made his mystery known to us

† His mystery is salvation through Jesus' atonement

† We could never earn his forgiveness

† We were alienated from God

† We are rescued by his grace through our faith

† We have been created as God's masterpiece

† We have been made to do good works

† We are being built up with all other believers

† We are made one in Christ

† We have bold, confident, direct access to God

You will find it very encouraging to study the verses that bridge these two prayers. As in the first prayer, this second prayer has been interpreted differently, depending on the translators. Some take this passage as having multiple requests, which is not inherently incorrect. The original wording is quite technical, which makes it difficult to know for certain. However, due to the close connection between the various phrases in both prayers and how these two prayers parallel the one in Colossians 1:9-12 (which was also written while Paul was in a Roman prison), it is most helpful to understand this second Ephesian prayer as having one request with three results, just like the first prayer.

The Launchpad

The Spirit inspired Paul with very descriptive words in this beautifully worded, second Kingdom Come Prayer in Ephesians 3:14-19.

For this reason I bow my knees before the Father, from whom every family in heaven and on earth is named, that according to the riches of his glory he may grant you to be strengthened with power through his Spirit in your inner being, so that Christ may dwell in your hearts through faith - that you, being rooted and grounded in love, may have strength to comprehend with all the saints what is the breadth and length and height and depth, and to know the love of Christ that surpasses knowledge, that you may be filled with all the fullness of God.

The introduction to the prayer is: *For this reason I bow my knees before the Father, from whom every family in heaven and on earth is named.* For what reason? Why did Paul and his team focus so much of their time and emotional energies on praying for the believers in the various churches? The reason is God has done a marvelous thing in rescuing people out of the dark domain and bringing them together, into his Son's kingdom, as his people. He knows each one's name and he knows their family's names. God's calling is very individualistic - by specific names. Each person is called out, by name, to become part of this gigantic and hugely diverse family. He knows us all by name!

Direct Access

Prior to these verses, the apostle wrote another amazing truth: *in whom we have boldness and access and confidence through our faith in him.* The "whom" and the "him" are of course, Jesus Christ. What this doctrine declares is every believer has direct access to God the Father with bold assurance and unwavering confidence. We can be sure he hears us and acts according to what is best for us and his kingdom. The Father listens to our prayers and works accordingly because we are in his Son. We are in a forever union with him. Because we belong to Jesus, we can run to the Father at any time and tell him what's wrong. He always listens to his children!

The apostle also wrote he bowed down to pray. This doesn't mean bowing is the only stance we should take when praying. In Paul's day, the normal stance for praying was standing up. The Spirit influenced Paul and his team to often kneel when they prayed as a practical way of demonstrating their humility before God and their passion for the people for whom they were praying. Their commitment to these believers and deep dependence on their Lord frequently drove them to their knees for prayer. If you are part of a leadership team, occasionally kneeling as you intercede may be helpful.

Let me suggest you practice different positions when praying. Of course, you can pray anywhere and at any time. You can pray in the car or in a crowd. In the mornings, I usually sit on our sofa with a cup of coffee to read and pray. But we can learn much from our Savior by observing he often found a place to be alone to pray. Sometimes Jesus prayed looking up to his Father in the heavens. In his most desperate prayer, Jesus began praying on his knees, but when he was overcome with grief, fell face down to beg for his Father's help (Luke 22:42 and Matthew 26:39). Here in Ephesians, we read that Paul and his team often bowed in prayer. If you're the senior leader, have your team kneel to pray on occasion. There's no way that's right or wrong. It is good to change it up and it is good to let your body respond to what your heart is feeling. In my most challenging or depressing times, I have found that kneeling when I pray helps me to express my desperate dependence on my Father in the heavens. I felt like my leadership team took on a more revered attitude when we prayed together on our knees. Let your body position and your attitude in prayer reflect your love and reverence for God and your deep dependence on him.

Because we have bold access with confidence, Paul bowed and prayed to the Father: *from whom every family in heaven and on earth is named*. Prayers are very personal. We are praying to our Father whose people span the entire history of mankind. Heaven is filled with worshipping saints who have gone before us and with whom we all share a common lineage. We're all the children of God, one family from many different families and many different ethnicities, all of which are named by God himself. There is no place for prejudices in the family of God. No person is better than any other and no family is more important than any other family. Maybe you've heard it said, the ground is level at the foot of the cross. That's what the Apostle Paul reiterated here.

The Request

The second Kingdom Come Prayer request is this: *that according to the riches of his glory he may grant you to be strengthened with power through his Spirit in your inner being*. This is the request your Father longs to be asked. He wants you to ask him to strengthen those you lead with power through his Spirit in the depth of their being. This is his will for each saint, so according to Jesus' promise, the Father will answer the request. It's that simple.

Notice how Paul added the conditional clause to this strengthening by God. He was reminded by the Spirit to state the source of our power. What is this source? How are we empowered? The source is the riches of his glory. This phrase encapsulates the fullness and completeness of all of his attributes. God's desire is to apply all of his rich attributes in power to us for our spiritual transformation and mind renewal. It takes the power of God working mightily in our lives to bring about the changes he so desires. He uses two words for power to emphasize how much strengthening we really need. Paul prayed for those under his leadership *to be strengthened with power through his Spirit.*

It's a Gift

There's another critical emphasis in this prayer request. Empowerment is a *gift.* Paul didn't just pray that believers would be strengthened with power through the Spirit, although it's fine to ask in that way. Paul was led by the Spirit to ask specifically for God to *grant* this to happen. The word used here is the normal Greek word "to give." The noun form is "gift." The Spirit is emphasizing that this strengthening is a gracious gift from God. It is a gift he wants to give us as we ask and continue asking. It is so important for us to understand the Spirit led Paul to use the word "gift" a dozen times in this short letter. The Spirit is a gift (1:17), God's grace is a gift (3:2, 7, 8; 4:7, 8, 29), and his strengthening is a gift (3:16). Why does the Bible emphasize everything good we have is a gracious gift from God?

Too many times we slip back into the performance mindset that if we live just right or serve in Children's Ministries or give enough money to the church, God will give us his blessings. You can never earn God's blessings or his favor. You will never deserve them either. Our glorious heavenly Father gives us his grace and his power out of his steadfast love for us, *according to the riches of his glory*. As you ask God to strengthen you, always remember it is his gift to you. You don't deserve his empowerment, and you can't limit his strengthening by your failings.

We can migrate to either end of a faith-killing continuum: to think we deserve his grace or to think we're so weak in our faith he'll never bless us. You are his child. Our Father wants his children to understand all they will ever need comes from his hands. He wants to give us everything that will be good for us and his kingdom. Therefore, ask him. Ask him to make your church strong in his power through his Spirit. Ask and keep on asking. You may not see him answer immediately, which is why you must be diligent in your asking. God is faithful. His love for you and them is steadfast and independent of performance.

The first request in Ephesians 1:17 is for God to give his Spirit so he is known and understood better and better. The second request in 3:16 is for God to give his power through his Spirit so his people will be empowered through their union with him. Imagine the difference in the lives of those you lead if they're constantly being strengthened by the indwelling Spirit of Christ.

From the Inside Out

The fulfillment of the New Covenant, promised by the prophets of old, became reality in Christ: *Therefore, if anyone is in Christ, he is a new creation. The old has passed away; behold, the new has come* (2 Corinthians 5:17). Christ lives in and through us. He is our source of life and our strength to live: *I have been crucified with Christ. It is no longer I who live, but Christ who lives in me. And the life I now live in the flesh I live by faith in the Son of God, who loved me and gave himself for me* (Galatians 2:20). We have our identity in Christ, and he is our new life, our real life: *For you have died, and your life is hidden with Christ in God* (Colossians 3:3). The old nature is gone. All of these are astounding truths that are sometimes tough to grasp. That is why we need more of God's limitless power working within so we can believe all of these realities of God and live them out on a consistent basis.

The needed changes in our attitudes, actions, and allegiance take place deep within our souls. Our transformation process is an inside-out revolution that happens by God's gracious power working within us. He gives us strength to deny temptations. He empowers us to be able to understand how to apply his Word to our lives. He makes us mighty in faith to stand on biblical convictions when others deny him. He strengthens us to be able to follow him as he leads us to do his kingdom work. He empowers spouses to hang in there when the marriage seems hopeless. He strengthens his people to endure with patience all kinds of hardships, hurts, and disappointments. Our actions are reflective of what is happening in our heart. That is why Paul was inspired to ask God to give his people power through the Spirit deep within their very core.

The Need For Power

My wife, Tammy, and I had achieved the Great American Dream – our own business, a house, two cars, two kids and a dog. We were fairly mature in our faith and continuing to grow in our understanding of God's will for our lives. But the day I came home from work and Tammy told me she felt like God was calling us to be missionaries – I mean, the kind of missionary who goes to a foreign county to live – well, I just about dropped dead. I rationalized she must have gotten overly emotional at her women's Bible study (which was led by a missionary) and this totally insane idea would soon pass. "Make it go away God! Please, please, please change her mind." was my plea.

We committed to praying diligently about this for the next month. At that time, I was not familiar with the Kingdom Come Prayers, but I did understand how to ask him for his will and to give us clarity and unity. What I didn't realize was God was working powerfully within me to change my heart and to give me the strength to say "yes" to this terrifying assignment. His power within the depths of my soul was completely overwhelming. Within a month, I was convinced God did indeed want us to sell the business, our home, give up our bright financial future, and go to seminary to prepare to minister wherever in the world it was he planned for us to go. After completing seminary, we spent six years in Senegal, West Africa, with the mission organization SIM, sharing the fantastic news of forgiveness in Jesus Christ to the Muslims of that country, in their native language. Talking about power! He strengthened us to learn an African language so we could explain to them the wonderful reality of Jesus' sacrifice for our sins. That, my friend, is the power of God working in the depths of the heart of his children!

Being strengthened to answer "yes" to a missionary calling certainly isn't the norm. God's normal activity is to empower us daily to do the regular work of the Kingdom, like forgiving someone, showing patience, loving the unlovable, putting others ahead of ourselves, and sharing our possessions. The power of God is displayed through the kinds of attitudes and actions it produces in the hearts of his people as told so graphically in Jesus' story of the sheep and the goats in Matthew 25:31-46. When you experience the impact, or fruit, of the Spirit in your life, it is because the power of God gives you the strength to display these qualities. Sometimes, God gives us this internal strengthening without us even asking for it. That is how his grace works. However, his will for us is that we *ask* to have his power working within. He wants this people to live in the consciousness of knowing how much we need his strength deep within our souls. Once a person realizes their need for his power, they will keep asking. Once a leader pleads for his or her people to be empowered, he or she will continue asking because of the tangible impact it will produce.

Inner Being vs Old Self

In Chapter 7 of the letter to the church in Rome, the Apostle Paul was led by the Spirit to explain the internal war that happens in every believer. *So I find it to be a law that when I want to do right, evil lies close at hand. For I delight in the law of God, in my inner being, but I see in my members another law waging war against the law of my mind and making me captive to the law of sin that dwells in my members. Wretched man that I am! Who will deliver me from this body of death* (Romans 7:21-24)? Don't you connect with how Paul felt? As long as we live in these mortal bodies, we will always struggle with this war that rages within our hearts and minds. Our *new* heart wants to do what is right and to follow Jesus. However, the body we inhabit was born in sin and is embedded with sin. In addition to our sin problem, evil forces on the outside try to persuade us to reject Jesus' ways. We desperately need the power of God to win the daily battles. We know we will win the war in the end, but it's those constant skirmishes and personal struggles against sin and evil we can win with God's powerful help, as we ask.

Later in Ephesians, Paul wrote some scary stuff: *We do not wrestle against flesh and blood, but against the rulers, against the authorities, against the cosmic powers over this present darkness, against the spiritual forces of evil in the heavenly places* (6:12). Yikes! That's terrifying. You may have read Frank Peretti's novels, written in the late 80's and 90's, that portrayed fictionally how these evil forces might work. The first novel was titled after this verse, *This Present Darkness.* Peretti helped us to comprehend what might be happening in the spirit world around us, but it was scary reading. I'm so glad we can't see what's happening in the unseen world. But we don't need to be afraid. The answer to overcoming their influence was given in 6:10: *Finally, be strong in the Lord and in the strength of his might. Put on the whole armor of God, that you may be able to stand against the schemes of the devil.* This is a command. It's not a suggestion or a recommendation. Why? Because we desperately need the strength of his might. No one you are leading can be powerful enough in their own strength. But they can experience all the power they need as you intercede, asking the Father to give them his strength.

Have you noticed when the apostle wrote about the power of God that he used multiple words to describe it? We looked at this trifecta of power words in the third result of the first Kingdom Come Prayer in Chapter 3. Remember, the Spirit of God inspired the writers to use very specific words when they wrote the Bible. Paul used multiple words for power to help us understand just how much we need this completely limitless strength of God in our lives. The Spirit's purpose was to envision for us that God's magnificent power is available to his people, as we ask him for it. His Spirit comes along beside us and lives in us to strengthen us to love God with all our heart, soul, mind, and might.

Examples of Strengthening

I have made a concerted effort to gain control over my temper while driving. I have in no way "arrived", but I'm making progress. Do you have that temptation too? Apparently, a lot of drivers do. I've always been reluctant to put a Christian bumper sticker on my car due to my quick temper. What has made this especially challenging for me is drivers where I live have become significantly more selfish. The recent victories I've enjoyed have come from asking God to strengthen me in my inner being so I'll remain in control and not take the driving sins of others personally. If someone cuts me off or doesn't use their turn signal, I strive to let it go, by the power of God. My wife and I laugh about it as we sing Queen Elsa's famous chorus, "*Let it go, let it go...*". I can only let driving infractions go if I am conscious of God's power working in me. I know on my own, I'll probably lose my temper while driving. Every time I try on my own, I fail. When I ask God to give me his power to stay cool, calm, and collected, I'm better, much better. I can drive anger-free through Christ who strengthens me! And so can you.

We read the Apostle Paul had some kind of debilitating physical problem. He didn't tell us what the specific issue was, he just called it his *thorn in the flesh*. Like any of us would do, Paul pleaded with the Lord to take it away. But Jesus spoke to him and said: "*My grace is sufficient for you, for my power is made perfect in weakness*" (2 Corinthians 12:9). God's power in our lives doesn't mean every issue will be fixed the way we want it to be. On the contrary. The way we often experience the gracious power of God in our lives is when he sustains us through a very difficult time, when we realize we are weak. When we are in those tough times of life, we often cry out to God for his strength. But our Father wants us to learn to ask him for his power daily. He wants his children to realize their need of his mighty energy working within them each and every day, if they're going to live lives that are worthy of his calling. Paul experienced the grace of Jesus as he was strengthened by God's Spirit. As he recognized the limits of his personal strength and relied on God's power, he found he could overcome anything. And so can you. The people you lead can do all things through Christ who strengthens them as *you* ask the Father to give them his power through his Spirit in their heart and soul.

Let's now turn to the three results that flow out of asking the Father to make us mighty by his power through his Spirit in our inner being. As you read these results, keep in mind they all come from God giving his power to his people.

1st Result

The impact of asking the Father to give his strength through his Spirit is: *so that Christ may dwell in your hearts through faith—that you, being rooted and grounded in love* (Ephesians 3:17). As mentioned previously, the various English translations treat this part of the prayer differently. Some begin a new request in the middle of this sentence, asking for us to be rooted and grounded in love. The English Standard Version emphasizes the link between the clauses and the request. A literal translation of the original is: *that Christ may dwell through faith in your hearts, in love having been rooted and having been grounded.* I don't want to be too picky about the proper translation of this phrase. However, my experience in praying this prayer for many years is that expecting the result of Christ's abiding presence by asking for Spiritual strength is more practical. For the Lord Jesus to be at home in our emotions, desires, and dreams, it takes tremendous power from the Spirit of God working within a soul.

As Jesus is more and more at home in a believer's heart, they will become more and more rooted and grounded in his kind of love. This is a mind-boggling and very life-changing concept. Jesus can inhabit a follower's heart, through their faith, as God empowers them with his Spirit's strength. As they become more comfortable with Jesus' continual presence through his Spirit, his love is more established in their soul. They become a more loving person. Doesn't that make sense?

We've already looked at several Bible passages that teach us about the Spirit living within us. Jesus and his Spirit exist in such unity with the Father that it is absolutely correct to say Jesus lives in us. In actuality, Jesus is seated with his Father in the heavenlies. But, because he is completely one with the Spirit, even though it is the Spirit who inhabits us, the Bible rightly states that *Christ may dwell in your hearts*. Since the words were inspired by the Spirit as he breathed them out through the various writers, it is actually the Spirit himself who stated that Jesus dwells in our hearts. Have you noticed in the Bible how the Spirit rarely brought attention to himself? He inspired the writers to focus much more on the Father and the Son rather than on himself. He's almost the forgotten member of the Trinity. By the Spirit emphasizing the Father and the Son, we are given one more example of the depth of love and devotion each member of the Trinity has for the others.

The word "to dwell" means to inhabit or to be at home. The opposite of this word means to be a guest or a visitor. There is an ownership issue conveyed. Jesus comes in like he owns the place and has full reign over every room and every closet. A great little book came out in 1986 by RB Munger titled, *My Heart Christ's Home*. It's a best seller, and I highly recommend it. Munger symbolizes the rooms in a home as the areas within a believer's heart, to see if Jesus is really welcomed there and comfortable with all that goes on in that particular room. If you picture your heart or mind as a home with multiple rooms and closets, is there a place in your heart's home where Jesus has little influence? For most of us, we have a room or a closet or two where the Lord is kept off limits. Almost subconsciously, we live as if we can hide things from God. Nothing is hidden from his view. Our deepest thoughts and cravings are in vivid, HD clarity before him. Therefore, we need the power of God to help us to be able to open those locked doors, to clean out those sin-stained closets and invite Jesus to live there as a permanent resident.

Resident vs Guest

Another way to consider this illustration is to think about Jesus Christ as a guest or a roommate. Could your life be depicted as a home where Jesus is asked to come to dinner on occasion or invited over to hang out and watch the game? This is a powerful question to consider for those you have direct influence over. If our relationship to God is about going to a church service once a week, then Jesus is more of a guest that comes on Sundays rather than a welcomed roommate. Even for the most faithful followers, thinking about the reality of Jesus' presence in us every moment of every day is difficult to do. It takes the power of the Father, who gives us his strength through his Spirit, to keep us desiring his Son to be a cherished resident rather than an occasional guest.

As you read this, you may be convicted by the Spirit that he doesn't really feel at home in *your* heart. Are there areas of your life where you don't feel comfortable opening up to Jesus? Confess this sin and begin asking God to empower you so that Jesus can take up full residence in your heart. Ask the Father, according to his gloriously limitless might, to give you the power to open that locked room so you can work together to clean it out. You need the power of God to help you remove the things that you don't want Jesus to see, just like the members of your church do. We can all do this through Christ who is our strength. Once you make this a constant request for yourself, you are then in a perfect position to ask the same for your church members.

One more thing. You can't remove worn out furniture from a room and it be warm and cozy. It must be remodeled with new furniture. As we read earlier, we are to take off the old and put on the new. By the power of God, sinful habits can be replaced with righteous actions. I'm not only learning to not get angry at other drivers, I'm learning how to be a gracious driver. Looking at porn isn't solved by stopping the sin. A positive action must replace the negative one. Reading the Bible, listening to righteous music, reading Christian novels, or volunteering time are all positive ways to replace the sin of viewing porn. Gossiping has to be replaced with speaking the truth in love, by the power of God. Coveting is conquered when it is replaced with a sense of thankfulness and appreciation for what the Lord has given, and that includes possessions, abilities, circumstances, looks, talents, positions, jobs, and relationships. Transformation and renewal are made possible by the strength our Father longs to give as we ask him. The result will be a conscious awareness of Jesus abiding presence.

Through Faith

Let's now focus on two words in this statement that are pivotal: *through faith*. The first result of asking the Father to give his power is that Jesus dwells in a believer's heart through their faith. Our belief isn't based on feelings or emotions we conjure up. Our faith is based on fact. God says unequivocally he and the Son live within each believer through the Spirit. Again, we need to go back to the promise of the New Covenant. Hundreds of years before Jesus came to earth, God promised he would give his people a new spirit and a new heart. When you came to believe in Jesus as the Son of God who paid your ransom price, you were given his Spirit to live within you for the rest of your life. Jesus declared to his disciples on that Holy Thursday night the New Covenant was about to be ratified: *"If you love me, you will keep my commandments. And I will ask the Father, and he will give you another Helper, to be with you forever, even the Spirit of truth, whom the world cannot receive, because it neither sees him nor knows him. You know him, for he dwells with you and will be in you"* (John 14:15-17).

Notice closely Jesus' words. He stated the Helper, the Holy Spirit, was *with* them. How did that work? Because Jesus lived *with* them, he could also say the Spirit lived *with* them. But something wonderful is about to happen. The age of the New Covenant is about to begin. That's why Jesus said in the next phrase the Helper, a very descriptive name for the Spirit, will be *"in you."* These two unique prepositions represent an amazing new era for mankind. Jesus, Emmanuel, God with us, has become God *in* us. Jesus' promise became reality when the Spirit first inhabited the 120 believers on the day of Pentecost in Acts Chapter 2. Think of the impact in your church members if they lived in the consciousness of their "Helper's" presence and power. Since faith is key, we can certainly ask for the Father to strengthen a believer's faith: *"I believe; help my unbelief!"* (Mark 9:24b)

Because God Said So

However, our experience is a lot of the time, we have little proof Jesus' Spirit is living in us. We don't feel like he's living within us. There's no outward sign. There's no inward sensation. Most of the time, the only way that we know the Spirit lives within is because God said so. Jesus promised you he is there and there is nothing in this world or the spirit world that can separate you from him: *For I am sure that neither death nor life, nor angels nor rulers, nor things present nor things to come, nor powers, nor height nor depth, nor anything else in all creation, will be able to separate us from the love of God in Christ Jesus our Lord* (Romans 8:38-39). Once he comes to live in a believer, he will never leave or vacate the premises. Jesus has promised that he is with us every step of the way, regardless of how we feel. That's why faith can't be based on feelings.

Are there times when you feel his presence? Sure. You know that's true. Are there times when others see the power of God working in and through you. Absolutely. But most of the time, it's a matter of faith. What exactly is faith in Jesus? *Now faith is the assurance of things hoped for, the conviction of things not seen* (Hebrews 11:1). Faith is the certainty that everything God has told us in his Bible is true. Faith convicts us that even though we can't see the presence of Jesus living in us through his Spirit, he is there.

Rooted and Grounded

The result of Christ taking up permanent residency is his love will be more and more the basis and foundation of a person's life. There are two descriptive illustrations in the phrase *rooted and grounded in love*. On the one hand, we will become rooted in our faith like a huge oak tree is rooted in the ground. No matter how much the winds of hardships blow, our love will hold fast, because our roots of faith will extend down deep within Jesus soil of sacrificial love. Jesus' love can also be depicted as the strong foundation of a well-built building. Picture a concrete and steel structure whose foundation reaches deep into the earth so it can weather the strongest tornado or Category 5 hurricane.

The kind of love we're being rooted and grounded in has three dimensions. It is the steadfast love Jesus has for us as his brothers and sisters. It is also the love we have for Jesus, his Father, and the Spirit. And it is the love we believers have for one another. This is the love that will drive you as a leader to intercede for those you can influence. The context of this prayer, and the entire letter to the church in Ephesus, spells out all three dimensions of Jesus' love.

God strengthening us in our inner being means Jesus will be more at home in our hearts. We'll be more aware of his constant presence. We'll no longer try to hide things from him (as if we could hide anything from Jesus). We'll stop trying to pretend he doesn't know everything we're up to. As we get more comfortable with the Spirit's power through his presence, we'll love the Lord with greater devotion. We'll also begin to understand how great his love is for us. And most importantly, we'll begin to love people in our church, as well as all other believers, with more depth and consistency. That's what it means to be rooted and grounded in agapé love. And this rooting and grounding comes about as we ask the Father to empower us and those we lead.

Jesus' Kind of Love

What is agapé love? Jesus took an ordinary Greek word and exploded it into the rich reality of his kingdom. "Agapé" was an ancient word that was different from the more popular words used in those days for romantic love and brotherly love. It was used primarily to describe the Greek gods. In Greek mythology, agapé was the word used for the love the gods chose to give to certain people, especially rulers and generals. Jesus took this word and gave it new power and a much fuller meaning. The forgiveness of sins he purchased releases a whole new kind of love, agapé love, that overflows, fills and directs all of life, thoughts and actions. We have no equivalent English word. The closest is "altruism." How often do you hear that word used? Right. Only if you're taking the SAT.

I love fried chicken. I don't eat it as often as I used to because so many people say that it isn't healthy. I love the phrase, "Eat Mor Chikin!" I also love football. I love the beach and the mountains. I love my wife, Tammy, our children, their spouses (yes, I really do!), and I love the Lord Jesus. Now how in the world can one word adequately express my feelings for fried chicken, football, my wife, and my Lord?

Agapé love is how Jesus explained his Father's mercy toward us: "*For God so loved* (agapé-d) *the world, that he gave his only Son, that whoever believes in him should not perish but have eternal life. For God did not send his Son into the world to condemn the world, but in order that the world might be saved through him* (John 3:16-17). God agapé loved us before we ever returned that love. He agapé loves us with such magnitude we could never adequately reciprocate it. That is the basis of agapé love – it doesn't require reciprocation. It's not a tit-for-tat that if you love me, I'll love you back. Agapé love has a price. Agapé love always costs the giver. It is a selfless love that focuses completely on the receiver, not the giver. A stunning example of agapé love happened when Jesus was on the cross: *"Father, forgive them, for they don't know what they are doing"* (Luke 23:34 - NLT). Isn't it true we're often hurt by people who don't really know what they are doing? Stop and think about that question before continuing.

I wonder if the greatest challenge you face is the same one I struggle with – agapé loving every other believer the same way Jesus agapé loves them. People can be so annoying. They can be so different in their thinking. People, especially God's people, seem to have so many little quirks. Many of them just seem downright weird. And some personalities rub me the wrong way. I sometimes find it easier to love those who are far from God than the saints who are adopted into the family with me. Can you relate?

Freely Receive, Freely Give

Jesus made it crystal clear: *This is my commandment, that you love one another as I have loved you.* (John 15:12) The old apostle John hammered this commandment in all of his writings. It couldn't be any clearer. Our highest responsibility in the kingdom of God is to agapé love all of those God has called into his kingdom, every last one of them, no matter what. What is needed is a constant plea to God to empower us so that we can keep Christ at home in our hearts and be rock-solid in our agapé love for him and for all of his people. This is why Kingdom leaders pray Kingdom Come Prayers!

When that church member or fellow ministry leader you don't particularly like says or does something that grates against your nerves, it's time to cry out to the Father for his power so that both of you can agapé love each other. Realize that your relationship with another believer is never one-on-one. Christ is always there. He lives in you and the other believer through his Spirit. The more I remind myself of this truth, especially when I'm ticked off by a fellow follower, it changes how I feel about them. I find that asking the Father to grant me to be strengthened helps me to live in the consciousness of his presence, which gives me more incentive to agapé love like he does and pray for them. We are all in desperate need of the Father to strengthen us so we can take direct control of our thinking, to turn it to agapé love.

When Jesus is at home in our thoughts and emotions, we can be very open and honest with our Father. The more honest we are, the deeper our relationship becomes. Isn't that true in all of your relationships with people? Sure it is, and it's the same way with your Father in the heavens. Anytime you are brutally honest with yourself about the things that really matter in life, you will realize your need for God's power. Maybe I should reword that. You will realize your desire for God's power. God's power is what you will begin to want more than anything, for yourself and for everyone you lead. The first result that comes from asking the Father to give his power through his Spirit deep within the soul is Christ's welcomed residency that grounds all of life in agapé love.

Got Christ? Ask your Father, according to the vast treasures of his magnificent splendor, to give those you lead his mighty power through his Spirit in their inner self so that their faith in Jesus' abiding presence makes agapé love flourish.

2nd Result

So that we *may have strength to comprehend with all the saints what is the breadth and length and height and depth, and to know the love of Christ that surpasses knowledge.* This is the second result of the Father giving his power to his children. We will have the power that's needed to understand the full volume of the agapé love of Jesus. This result takes the understanding of agapé love to immeasurable new heights. Let's dive into what this will look like in those you are privileged to lead.

Do we understand the full dimensions of Christ's love? Of course not, not completely. This understanding comes to a believer by asking the Father to give his power through his Spirit in the inner self. Stop and ponder what the Spirit meant when he led Paul to write such a statement - *the breadth and length and height and depth, and to know the love of Christ that surpasses knowledge.* What image comes to mind when you think about how broad and long and high and deep the love of Jesus is? What is the Spirit trying to help us see?

He inspired Paul to describe the fullness of Jesus' love as having four dimensions. What in the world is 4D? It's beyond our world. The fullness of Jesus' love is so great it is in an entirely different realm from our 3D world. Can anyone understand it fully? Not yet. The cross is the proof of the full volume of Jesus' love for his Father, for us, and the Father's love for the world.

Therefore be imitators of God, as beloved children. And walk in love, as Christ loved us and gave himself up for us, a fragrant offering and sacrifice to God (Ephesians 5:1-2). In giving up his holy life as the sacrifice and atonement for our sins, Jesus demonstrated his voluminous love for his people, his unwavering devotion to his Father, and his Father's sacrificial love for rebellious people. To have the power to comprehend the magnitude and dimensions of the love of Jesus, we must consider the breadth, length, depth, and height of his sacrifice.

Limitless Love

The love of Jesus and his willingness to be made sin on our behalf has no limits. He took on your sins and my sins and was punished by his Father for each of our sin crimes. His love reaches out widely to every person who is willing to accept it. There is no one so evil the love of Jesus can't penetrate his or her heart. Jesus suffered from the breadth and length and height and depth of the sins of mankind – every sin imaginable. His love is so broad that it surpasses all of those sins. The volume of his love is able to contain and to atone for all of the atrocities of mankind, every rebellious act against his Father. There is no sin that can't be covered over, except the sin of rejecting his forgiveness. You probably know the illustration parents sometimes use – stretching their arms as wide as possible and saying, "I love you *this* much!" That's the breadth of Jesus' love. He stretched his arms as widely as possible and allowed Roman soldiers to impale them to a cross beam to demonstrate his love for his Father, and for us.

Jesus' love is also long. We know the length of his love because we have all made him wait, possibly for years and years, before we confessed our sins and received his love. His waiting is not over once we finally accept his love and receive him as our Lord. He will continue to show us the length of his love as he waits for us to turn from that reoccurring sin or to serve where he's been trying to lead us. Jesus will have to wait, maybe a long time, for you to forgive someone who owes you. His love for us is so very long.

His love for us is high enough to overcome every rejection there is, because his love is the same as his Father's love. His Father gave his best to mankind, so the Son does the same. The height of the love of Jesus stretches the expanse of the universe. There is no limit. And the depth of Jesus' love knows all of our deepest secrets, the things we wouldn't dare tell our spouse or closest friend. He knows all of our thoughts and those dreams that wake us up in a cold sweat, and he loves us anyway. The Lamb of God loves us in spite of all of the sin we carry within. He loves us even when we deny our love for him and act like we don't belong to him. This is the breadth, the length, the height, and the depth of the love of God, which is in Christ Jesus our Lord. This is agapé love.

How will his people ever have the strength to understand the full volume of the love of Jesus? It will come as the Father is asked to give his power to his people deep within their souls. Our Father wants us to know his Son's love that, oddly enough, is actually beyond knowing. What in the world does that mean?

Christ's love surpasses knowledge because humans can never completely understand the full extent of the

Son's love, at least not on this side of eternity. When we are with him, in his visible presence, we will know and experience the fullness of his love. From the way Jesus prayed in John 17, it sounds as if he can't wait to show us the full extent of his love in his glory. But human eyes and hearts can't absorb it. Only when he has made us immortal can we take in the vastness of his love. But until that day comes, we must ask and keep asking our Father to empower those we lead.

All the Saints

The final part of this second result shows us how important the local church is to us and to Christ. Again, the result is that you: *may have strength to comprehend with all the saints what is the breadth and length and height and depth, and to know the love of Christ that surpasses knowledge.* We have yet to consider the phrase, *all the saints.* Remember this is a letter to the church in the city of Ephesus. Back in those days, there was typically only one church in each city.

The love of Christ is to be understood by all believers, the saints. Paul didn't pray, and neither should we, that only certain individuals would be strengthened by God to be strong enough to comprehend Christ's love. He asked that everyone in the Ephesian church would experience his gigantic agapé love. He goes on to explain in Ephesians 4 the church is paramount in God's rescue mission. The only way an individual believer can grow in their faith, live in a way that is worthy of their calling, and comprehend the love of Jesus is in relationship with other believers. The church is Jesus' bride. The church is what Jesus is building. Your church can know the fullness of his agapé love by experiencing it through other followers who are demonstrating it.

The love of Jesus is both his love for his Father and his love for his people. We've already looked at his highest command, that we are to emulate his love for his people. Because we are all called the beloved, we are to agapé love each other in the same way that Jesus loves us. He loves us when we don't love him back. So agapé love is never conditional. It doesn't wait until the person in your home group, work team, or elder board asks for forgiveness. Agapé love extends forgiveness before it is ever deserved, which is the love of Christ the Father wants us to know *and* experience. If it is beyond knowing, that means it must be understood and experienced. Agapé love goes beyond the knowledge of another believer's faults, sins, and imperfections. Despite all that is known about another believer and the terrible things they've done, our calling is to agapé love them because Jesus loves them unconditionally. This kind of response seems almost impossible, but it's not only possible, the Father expects it. And this love is achieved through the power of God working in his people. We are all desperately dependent on our Father's help.

How are things going in your church? In your ministry? Got strife? Are there broken relationships? Any squabbling on the elder or deacon teams? What should you do when there is? Pray like crazy! Ask your Father in the heavens that according to the riches of his glory he will empower everyone in your church with strength through his Spirit, so that everyone is rooted and grounded in agapé love. Then your church can begin to have the strength to understand how Jesus' love is so much bigger than their silly differences like the type of music that is played, the length of the sermons, how announcements are handled, or how frequently you celebrate the Lord's Supper.

Pastors, church leaders, and worship directors, please pray this way! Praying regularly and passionately these Kingdom Come Prayers for your entire church family is very likely the best thing you can do for them. If Paul and his team never stopped praying this way for all the churches they led, you certainly are called by God to do the same for the one church you lead.

In one of the churches I was privileged to pastor, the elders and I were led by the Spirit to pray specifically and regularly for our church family. We took the entire membership and divided them among the days of the week so we could pray together for each person and each family using these Kingdom Come Prayers. We informed the church family how we were praying for them, just as Paul did. Each week, praying separately, the elders and I used one of Paul's Kingdom Come Prayers to intercede for those under our leadership. Great things happened. The elders more clearly understood their calling as co-shepherds who were responsible for the spiritual growth of the members. The church family felt cared for and were inspired to pray similarly for their families and fellow church members. Unity and maturity ensued.

Imagine the impact if outsiders in your community saw churches coming together in the love of Jesus? What if ministries and churches began much greater collaboration? Think about the impact of your leadership board truly loving one another selflessly. Isn't it time for an Agapé Love Revolution in our churches and ministries?

Our Father wants all of his children to be so connected with the indwelling Holy Spirit that the love of Jesus for us, our love for him, and our love for one another will saturate every desire and every action. Is it possible? It is by asking according to God's will!

3rd Result

The prayer crescendos into an almost inconceivable truth in the final result: *that you may be filled with all the fullness of God.* Yep, you need to read that one again. This is God's intended outcome when we ask for his strengthening. This is the goal of salvation for our lives on earth – that Christ is fully formed in us. Really? A person can be filled with all of God's fullness? Not really. Jesus was, of course. He was the fullness of God's deity in human form. And you and I certainly aren't Jesus. So, what does this crescendo mean for us?

The words *"filled"* and *"fullness"* come from how the Greek-speaking people in the first century described a ship. When all of the sailors, the rowers, the soldiers, the supplies, and the cargo were on board, the ship was then "full." For us, it's the picture of a plane with all the crew members, passengers, luggage, and any freight, plus the tanks are full of fuel and the galley is full of snacks and drinks - then the plane is full.

The fullness of God is the totality of his attributes that can be given to his people, like the fruit of the Spirit – love, joy, peace, patience, kindness, goodness, faithfulness, gentleness, and self-control. Not included in this list of attributes is God's wisdom, knowledge, and power. Since the fullness of God was in the man Jesus Christ, we can look to Jesus to understand God's goal for his people in this process of continual transformation. He wants the nature of his Son fully formed within us so we are mature in Christ.

A Full Group

But no person, except of course for Jesus, could possibly contain the fullness of all that God is. The fullness of God is how he makes his power and his presence visible to the world. As we experience God doing in us and through us what we could never do on our own, we are being filled with his grace. But no single human can have all of God's holiness, power, and wisdom. The fullness of God is experienced in his local churches, among the gathered saints who are learning and experiencing the full volume of the love of Christ together. Paul was praying for the church in Ephesus.

We tend to read this prayer as if it is meant for us as individual believers. Remember, first and foremost this letter and the prayer within it are for his gathered believers, Christ's church. To be filled with God's fullness is to be filled up to all the measure of God's fullness that is on display in the church. It is God's power and love he wants to pour out on his people through his people. This is more easily understood as we continue reading in Ephesians. From this prayer, Paul was led to write about why the church exists and how it is intended to work. In Ephesians 4, he described a unified group of followers of Jesus who are all doing their part, according to their Spiritual giftedness, to build each other up: *until we all attain to the unity of the faith and of the knowledge of the Son of God, to mature manhood, to the measure of the stature of the fullness of Christ* (4:13).

One person cannot have all the attributes of God. One person can't display all of the love and power of Jesus. The diversity of how God gives individuals Spiritual gifts is evidence of our dependence on one another. God's fullness is manifested through his church as each person is learning how to be who God has rebirthed them to be and serving accordingly. It takes the whole church together, the community of believers, with all of their diversities, gifts, talents, passions, and experiences to demonstrate the fullness of Jesus Christ, as they are continuously being strengthened by the Father.

Growing Up Together

The verses that follow the prayer tell us how this happens: *Rather, speaking the truth in love, we are to grow up in every way into him who is the head, into Christ, from whom the whole body, joined and held together by every joint with which it is equipped, when each part is working properly, makes the body grow so that it builds itself up in love.* (4:15-16)

Don't miss the key. Each part is working properly. That means each member of your church is growing together in their knowledge of God and in his power working within them (another clear reason why the leaders of a church must pray diligently for each person who calls the church home). If each person is working properly, they are serving in the area where they can make the greatest contribution to the whole. It does not mean Alicia gets to sing on the Praise Team, even though she can't ever find the right key because she makes up her own. It definitely does not mean David should teach a class when he's the only person in the church who thinks he's a good teacher. It does mean the truth about life and Christ is spoken in agapé love to one another. As the church is firing on all cylinders, everyone is built up in love and grows into a mature, fully grown-up Jesus.

The prayer request is for everyone in the church in to be empowered by God's Spirit so that Christ can be at home in their hearts so they can comprehend together the vastness of his love, experiencing it in all its fullness. Then, as a group they can be filled with all of God's fullness. God wants to receive glory through his people, collectively, as they experience his fullness and grow accordingly, at each one's individual pace.

But is all of this really possible? The prayer is so magnificent and so different from how we typically pray. Can a local church or a core group of followers in a ministry really be filled with God's fullness like this? Can believers be so empowered by God that Jesus is at home in their hearts so they are experiencing more and more of his limitless love?

But Wait, There's More

Immediately following Paul's magnificent request is this incredible blessing in 3:20-21: *Now to him who is able to do far more abundantly than all that we ask or think, according to the power at work within us, to him be glory in the church and in Christ Jesus throughout all generations, forever and ever. Amen.*

God knew full well you and I would wonder whether this prayer could become reality. He knows that we doubt. We don't doubt whether he can or wants to bring these kinds of changes. We doubt whether he will do it through us or in our people. "I know God can definitely do it, but can he really do it in us and through me?" That's why the Spirit led Paul to conclude the prayer with this staggering blessing in the *middle* of his letter. That's not where you are supposed to put the blessing or benediction (a fancy word for blessings). Why is it in Chapter 3 rather than at the end of Chapter 6? Because our loving Father knew we needed this incredibly inspiring truth to follow such a grandiose prayer.

Now to him who is able...You are not able. You can't do any of these things. You are not able to empower yourself or inspire others to be grounded in agapé love or grasp the full volume of the love of Jesus. God is able. He is so able he has the ability to do infinitely more than what is even in this prayer. Each time you pray to the Father, he is able to far surpass what you prayed and even what you weren't brave enough to pray. How is he able to do even the unthinkable?

He is able because it's *his* power at work within us. Notice it's "us" and not "me" or "you". God is able to do all of these amazing things through his power that is working in and through all of his people collectively. If you weren't sure whether this was all about God working through his church, just read what follows that phrase: *to him be glory in the church and in Christ Jesus throughout all generations, forever and ever. Amen.* God wants to be glorified in his churches, in his people gathered in communities, by what they are doing and how they are demonstrating the agapé love of Jesus. To be glorified means that he is getting all of the credit for all of the good that is taking place. When people outside the Kingdom see the good things happening and they inquire, then God can be given all the praise.

Don't ever forget God is able. He is able to do more amazing things than you can possibly comprehend. He is able to do these things because he is giving his people his power through his Spirit, grounding and rooting them in agapé love. His desire is for his people to experience the same kind of love for one another that the Father, Son, and Spirit have for each other.

May this reality fuel your desire to pray passionately and persistently for what God wants to do in and through the saints you were called to lead.

Use this first-person version of the second Kingdom Come Prayer on page 111 to help you memorize it. Tear it out of the book so you can keep it with you as a reminder of how to ask God to strengthen everyone you lead.

Kingdom Come Prayer #2

Ephesians 3:16-19

THE REQUEST

Dear Father in the heavens, I ask that out of your glorious riches you will grant the saints that I lead to be strengthened with your power through your Spirit in their inner most being...

1st Result

so that you, Lord Jesus, will be more at home in their hearts through faith, making them rooted and grounded in agapé love...

2nd Result

so that they will have strength together to understand how wide and high and long and deep your love is Jesus, experiencing it beyond knowledge...

3rd Result

so that together, they will be filled with all of your fullness.

Chapter 5 – Ask for Love

And it is my prayer that your love (agapé) *may abound more and more, with knowledge and all discernment, so that you may approve what is excellent, and so be pure and blameless for the day of Christ, filled with the fruit of righteousness that comes through Jesus Christ, to the glory and praise of God* (Philippians 1:9-11).

How do you know which of the Kingdom Come Prayers to pray? This third prayer helps us with that answer in a couple of ways. Knowing the context of each of the prayers is key. Learning certain things about each church as you read the specific letters will increase your understanding of the context. Each church had its unique set of circumstances and challenges, similar to every church that's ever existed. They all had their own issues, and each had a unique relationship with Paul. For an even fuller understanding of each of the Epistles, read how that specific church came about in Acts. For

113

example, we learn from Acts 16:6-10 of the unique way the Spirit of Jesus led Paul and his team to the region of Macedonia, where the ancient city of Philippi was located. The history of the birth of the Philippian church is captured in this same chapter. Paul was not able to remain in Philippi very long. In contrast, he spent three years with the church in Ephesus (Acts 20:31). Knowing these details gives us greater clarity to understand each of the Kingdom Come Prayers.

Did you notice how different the Philippian prayer is compared to the two in Ephesians? Even though Paul knew the church members in Ephesus much better than he did those in Philippi, the Philippian church had a special place in Paul's heart. He wrote: *For God is my witness, how I yearn for you all with the affection of Jesus Christ* (1:8). Paul wrote repeatedly in this letter of the joy they brought to his heart, because they were living out their faith so boldly. To the Ephesian church, Paul explained rich doctrinal truths that led to strong admonishments and cautions about living out their faith in righteous behavior. To the Philippians, the apostle focused more on praising and encouraging them to keep growing in their faith.

Maturity Differs

The Philippian letter reveals a church that is healthy and strong in their faith. Paul thanked them for their *partnership in the gospel* (1:5) and felt deeply about them because they were *partners* (1:7 HCSB) as they gave generously to meet Paul's needs (4:10-16). The church also prayed regularly for Paul and his team (1:19). The letter highlights their obedience (2:12) and maturity

(3:15). But it was their agapé-fueled generosity that was so incredibly palpable. You can read how Paul described their love in 2 Corinthians 8:1-5.

What can we learn from this church? The prayer request in Philippians 1:9 seems much more suited for followers who are a little further down the tracks. They were by no means perfect and they certainly had not "arrived". But their agapé love was tangibly sacrificial. It was a love that was willing to deliberately suffer in order to serve others.

A few paragraphs after the prayer, Paul wrote: *Therefore, my beloved, as you have always obeyed, so now, not only as in my presence but much more in my absence, work out your own salvation with fear and trembling, for it is God who works in you, both to will and to work for his good pleasure* (2:12-13). "Beloved" means: the ones who are agapé loved. Why does Paul feel this way about them? They are striving to obey all of Jesus' teachings because of their agapé love for the Lord. Can't you hear Paul cheering them on as they are seeking to serve Jesus and his people? Therefore, he reminded them it was God himself who was working in them to give them the desire to love and obey. And it was God himself who was working in them to give them the strength to do the things their faith was leading them to do. Therefore, this Kingdom Come Prayer is a request for those who are more mature in their faith. As we unpack this prayer, it will become more apparent why this request is especially powerful for those who are already faithful in expressing agapé love.

The Request

Like the prayers in Ephesians, this prayer has one request with multiple results. The request is: *And it is my prayer that your love may abound more and more, with knowledge and all discernment.* Paul continually asked that God would make their agapé love abound. This could not happen without his direct involvement. It's evident, from this letter and every letter Paul wrote under the Spirit's influence, each Christ-follower is desperately dependent on God.

Our heavenly Father wants us to ask him to make our agapé love abound more and more. If agapé love is flourishing more and more, then it's already present and active, just like it was in the believers in Philippi. Their agapé love inspired them to give extravagantly. The way it is worded in 2 Corinthians 8:1-5, it almost sounds as if they gave until they barely had anything left for themselves. Their agapé love was already prominent. Therefore, Paul and his team prayed it would overflow even more and even more beyond that. His vision was their agapé love would continue to increase in devotion to the Lord and to his people. This prayer request is for agapé love to fill the soul, so it splashes out on others.

Wouldn't it be cool if your gas tank could do that? You start out with half a tank, but the more you drive, the fuller it gets. As you continue driving, it keeps replenishing itself with more and more gas. You are using gas to drive, but your tank is being refilled with even more than your car is consuming. That's what God wants to do within our hearts with his agapé love.

Whose Love?

It seems as if the request should be for God to make *his* love increase and abound in us. Should it really be *our* agapé love that's increasing? Yes! The Spirit's inspired words tell us to pray for *our* agapé love to abound and overflow. Why *"our"* love?

God is love (1 John 4:8). He doesn't have love; it is who he is. The only agapé love you and I have in us is from God. As his born-from-above children, we have been regenerated and given a new heart of agapé love. Since the Spirit is in us, agapé love is in us. John wrote we have God's very seed in us (1 John 3:9). Since we are called to imitate God, we are called to agapé love like he does. It is our highest value and the most distinct characteristic of a follower of Jesus Christ. At least, it's supposed to be our most distinguishing characteristic. Jesus declared to his disciples on that Holy Thursday night: "*A new commandment I give to you, that you love one another: just as I have loved you, you also are to love one another. By this all people will know that you are my disciples, if you have love for one another* (John 13:34-35).

The old commandment was to love one another as yourself. It's called the Golden Rule. The new commandment is radically different. Maybe we should call it the Diamond Rule. Currently, a choice diamond is worth more than 200 percent of the same amount of gold. It's a good comparison between the new commandment love and the Golden Rule love. The new commandment means you care more for the other person than you do for yourself. That's agapé love. It is through loving others selflessly that we are identified as Jesus' people. Because agapé love is who Jesus is (note the personification of agapé love in 1 Corinthians 13), agapé love is to be who we are becoming. That's the love Jesus gave and continues to give to his people, through his Spirit, in their heart of hearts.

Our Greatest Need

The greatest need all believer's share is for agapé love to super-abound with increasing measure. Isn't this true in your life? May I answer that for you? Yes, it's true for you because it's true for me and every other believer walking on planet earth.

Paul cheered the Philippian church to even further acts of agapé love: *Therefore if you have any encouragement from being united with Christ, if any comfort from his love, if any common sharing in the Spirit, if any tenderness and compassion, then make my joy complete by being like-minded, having the same love, being one in spirit and of one mind. Do nothing out of selfish ambition or vain conceit. Rather, in humility value others above yourselves, not looking to your own interests but each of you to the interests of the others. In your relationships with one another, have the same mindset as Christ Jesus* (2:1-5, NIV).

The Spirit defined agapé love by stating that it is putting the interests of others above your own. Agapé love is humbling yourself and caring more about the other person than you do about yourself. It is agapé love that will empower you to wrestle in Kingdom Come Praying for your church family, just like Paul's team member, Epaphras (Colossians 4:12).

Believers can never have too much agapé love. What drives this request for the Kingdom to come about in the heart of a believer is the realization that agapé love is present but lacking. As agapé love is extended to others, a follower's agapé love tank needs to be replenished. Since our agapé love sometimes leaks, or even evaporates in stressful times, we all need a continual replenishing of his powerful love.

Up and Out

This request for an increasing flow of agapé love is multi-directional; it's up and out. God no doubt wants us to agapé love him more and more – no conditions. If life is good, we are lovingly devoted, and when life is tough and times are hard, we still love him with our whole being. The Spirit longs for our love for the Father, and the Son to continue in unwavering devotion. God's will is for our agapé love to overflow towards him in constant praise and thanksgiving.

His will is also that our agapé love will continue to overflow toward the people he loves so dearly and who he has placed in your circle of influence. It makes perfect Kingdom sense for agapé love to be the most prominent in the homes of his people, within our most intimate relationships. If you can't consistently extend agapé love to your spouse and children, how can your public acts of kindness and generosity truly be genuine agapé love? Imagine how God is glorified and pleased when agapé love pours out from his local churches into the schools, the neighborhoods, and the places of business where his people live, work, and study.

Full Knowledge

Let's take another look at the request: *And it is my prayer that your love may abound more and more, with knowledge and all discernment.* Agapé love doesn't abound more and more in gushy, handholding, Kumbaya love fests. Agapé love grows with full knowledge and keen discernment. The word for knowledge is the same word used in the first Kingdom Come Prayer from Ephesians 1:17-19. The unique thing about agapé love is that it abounds more and more in razor-sharp understanding and keen insights. Wise discernment to know what to do, what to say, and when to say it comes from agapé love that is on the increase.

You've experienced the tension and awkwardness of not knowing what to say or when to say it. Often the timing is more important than the words spoken. How do you avoid those relational potholes? Ask God to make your agapé love flourish in rich insights and keen discernment so you will know just how to respond and when to remain silent. This is an incredibly powerful request to make to the Father on behalf of those under your influence.

The Love Passage

We're told exactly what agapé love is in 1 Corinthians 13:1-8a. This passage is frequently used in wedding ceremonies, which is fine, but the context of the passage has to do with relationships within the church. In Chapters 12-14, Paul explained and illustrated that every church is stronger through the diversity of the people who make up the church and the way in which each individual makes their unique contribution to the whole. He was addressing the divisions that existed within that church. Paul emphasized the most important characteristic we possess is agapé love.

If I speak human or angelic languages

but do not have love,

I am a sounding gong or a clanging cymbal.

If I have the gift of prophecy

and understand all mysteries

and all knowledge,

and if I have all faith

so that I can move mountains

but do not have love, I am nothing.

And if I donate all my goods to feed the poor,

and if I give my body in order to boast

but do not have love, I gain nothing.

Love is patient, love is kind.

Love does not envy,

is not boastful, is not conceited,

does not act improperly,

is not selfish, is not provoked,

and does not keep a record of wrongs.

Love finds no joy in unrighteousness

but rejoices in the truth.

It bears all things, believes all things,

hopes all things, endures all things.

Love never ends. (1 Corinthians 13:1-8a, HCSB)

Did you notice how love is personified in this passage? That's because love *is* a person; God is love. He doesn't have love; he is love. Because the Spirit of God inhabits us, agapé love lives within. Like an apple tree producing delicious fruit, our agapé love needs to grow and keep on growing to have greater and wiser influence. Two tremendous results will be realized.

1ˢᵗ Result

Life is full of decisions. God wants you to ask for agapé love to overflow more and more *so that you may approve what is excellent and so be pure and blameless on the day of Christ.* (1:10) The word translated "approve" can also be translated discern, recognize, determine, choose, or see. God wants to help his people to be able to recognize the excellent choice. He wants to reveal, through agapé love, the superior option in every decision. The word translated "excellence" can also be translated best, superior, and important. Therefore, what happens to us as our agapé love increases with knowledge and all discernment is that we grow in our ability to recognize what is the excellent thing to do and to say. The most excellent option comes about through an ever-increasing agapé love growing within us.

Increasing agapé love allows us to be able to determine what is best in the heat of the battle. This prayer is my "go-to" flare prayer. When a harsh email arrives, an unkind word is spoken, or I feel disrespected, my greatest need is to be able to respond through the powerful wisdom of agapé love. Otherwise, I'll react from my old "Me Monster" self, and it will not be pretty. Been there, done that, got the trophy! That is why flaring a quick prayer request for agapé love to abound in you can produce just the right wisdom and discernment so you handle the situation in a Jesus-pleasing way.

The way to protect yourself, and those you lead, from being swayed by *rational lies* is to continually ask the Father to make agapé love overflow and abound so crystal, clear vision will reveal the best course of action to take. The love *of* Christ and love *for* Christ come to us through the indwelling Spirit of Christ so we can do what is excellent from Christ's perspective. Ask for it. That's how the Kingdom comes in you.

Excellence

Excellence isn't perfection. Excellence is giving our absolute best within the context of our current resources. It's leveraging all of the resources available: time, knowledge, product, talents, etc., to give one's best. Excellence honors God and inspires people.

You've been part of a worship service that you would describe as excellent. It wasn't flawless, but you had the sense that God was honored and those in attendance were inspired. A personal core value of excellence will help you to avoid the plague of mediocrity. We owe God our very best in everything we do.

That's why the Bible commands us: *And whatever you do, in word or deed, do everything in the name of the Lord Jesus, giving thanks to God the Father through him* (Colossians 3:17). Doing and saying excellent things in the name of the Lord Jesus means we're conscious of his presence, so we want to please him because he's watching and listening. Doing everything in the name of Jesus demands our best, given the time and energy we have for that specific task. Giving our best comes from a growing agapé love within us.

Giving your best means you give it all you have, regardless of who sees it or doesn't. In Ephesians 6:5-8, we are instructed to give our best in whatever we do as if Jesus himself is our boss. Therefore, increasing your agapé love can have a profound impact on how you lead your ministry. Praying for those you the more mature members of your church to have their agapé love increase will enable them to choose the most excellent way. Does someone you lead need a little pick-me-up in that arena? Then continue asking God to increase their agapé love more and more.

Thinking excellent thoughts is what Paul admonished the believers in Philippi to do: *Finally, brothers, whatever is true, whatever is honorable, whatever is just, whatever is pure, whatever is lovely, whatever is commendable, if there is any excellence, if there is anything worthy of praise, think about these things.* (Philippians 4:8) What is the best thing for you to be thinking about? It's beautifully described in this verse. How in the world can someone's thoughts consistently align with this list? The Father makes agapé love abound more and more, as we ask, and stinkin' thinkin' will be replaced with thoughts of truth, honor, justice, purity, loveliness, what is commendable, and all that is excellent. This is how you pray for yourself, so you'll be a high-impact Kingdom leader. It's also how you and your team can intercede for all the believers in your church or ministry, especially for those who are more mature, such as your volunteer leaders, teachers, and small group leaders.

Real Life Agapé

As an example, imagine a small group leader confides in you they are in a full-blown affair and they're contemplating leaving their spouse to run off with their new lover. You're completely caught off guard. What do you say? What questions can you ask to give them the right guidance? You know that God's will is one man, one woman, in a life-long covenant of marital fidelity. But how do you explain it? Ask God to make your agapé love overflow more and more so you'll have the wisdom to know the best thing to say at exactly the right time. Your abounding agapé love will take you to your knees to pray for him, asking God to flood his heart with the light of Christ so they can see their sin and the hurt and chaos they are causing. You continue praying for him and each time you see him at church, you fire off a flare prayer asking for your agapé love to overflow so you will know the best way to respond in each conversation. You trust God will give you the ability to determine when you need to confront him and how to encourage them to make the right choice. The Kingdom Come way is to keep praying for him and for yourself, that your agapé love will grow with knowledge and discernment so you can recognize what God wants you to do and say.

The Day

The result of praying for a growing agapé love isn't focused only on the here and now. The primary focus is on the day Jesus returns to earth. Let's consider it further: *so that you may approve what is excellent and so be pure and blameless on the day of Christ.* The day of Christ is the Second Coming, when Jesus will appear visibly to end all evil, judge the world, give us new immortal bodies, and create a new earth where we will live with him for an ageless age. Pretty good "day", huh?

Paul used the phrase two other times in this short letter. *I am sure of this, that he who began a good work in you will bring it to completion at the day of Jesus Christ* (Philippians 1:6). The excellent things their love and faith were driving them to do would be brought to full completion when Jesus returns. Paul encouraged them they were lights in the world who were *holding fast to the word of life, so that in the day of Christ* (2:16) he would be proud that his ministry with them was not in vain. The New Testament churches kept the reality of the return of Jesus in the forefront of their thinking and living. A growing agapé love for God will also bring about a more focused eternal perspective.

What if your church members, believing co-workers, or faithful team members truly lived out of an eternal perspective? A stronger focus on Jesus' return can be the norm through asking the Father to make agapé love grow and keep growing. As our love for God grows, our minds are opened up further to recognize what is excellent and to have a desire to live blamelessly before him. The first result from this Kingdom Come Prayer produces the ability to see what is best so we will live pure and blameless lives, because Jesus is coming back and his return is imminent. It could happen at any moment.

Here or There

Just after writing this prayer, Paul shared with the church in Philippi of his dilemma (1:19-26). His deep desire was to be with the Lord, which obviously meant he would have to die. He wasn't suicidal, he just knew how magnificently better life would be to live in Jesus' visible presence. Paul had faced death several times because of his faith in Christ. He knew living in the presence of Jesus, in the next life, far surpassed anything this life had to offer. He *really* knows that now! But he also wanted to continue his ministry here on earth, so he was torn, with one foot in this life and one foot in our real home.

Don't you want to have more of an eternal focus? Wouldn't it be so much more fun to know exactly how to respond to people in any given situation? And how might it impact your church or ministry if the more mature believers kept such an eternal focus? The opportunity for both of these is yours. "Dear Father, make *my* agapé love overflow more and more in full knowledge and complete discernment so that I can determine what is best and be pure and blameless until Jesus returns, diligently interceding for those under my care." But wait! There's more. A second result will come from this kind of praying.

2nd Result

The second result of asking your Father to make agapé love increase and keep growing is to be: *filled with the fruit of righteousness that comes through Jesus Christ, to the glory and praise of God.* One of Jesus' favorite metaphors was fruit. The word is used 66 times in 56 verses in the New Testament. All but 13 of those verses are in the Gospels. Jesus' audience was dependent on the crops and fruit that were harvested. From fig trees to grape vines, and wheat, the life-sustaining part of the plant was its fruit. That's why in Jesus day, fruit was so critically important to everyone. That's why Jesus frequently used the metaphor of their righteous character as being good fruit. We must bring his analogy to the 21st century and understand what *the fruit of righteousness* means for us today.

Jesus gave his most graphic illustration of fruit-bearing the night he was arrested. Try to picture our Lord walking along the road that night with his disciples when he comes to a lush vineyard, stops, and opens their minds, and now ours, to what happens when his kingdom becomes paramount.

"I am the true vine, and My Father is the vineyard keeper. Every branch in Me that does not produce fruit He removes, and He prunes every branch that produces fruit so that it will produce more fruit. You are already clean because of the word I have spoken to you. Remain in Me, and I in you. Just as a branch is unable to produce fruit by itself unless it remains on the vine, so neither can you unless you remain in Me.

I am the vine; you are the branches. The one who remains in Me and I in him produces much fruit, because you can do nothing without Me. If anyone does not remain in Me, he is thrown aside like a branch and he withers. They gather them, throw them into the fire, and they are burned. If you remain in Me and My words remain in you, ask whatever you want and it will be done for you. My Father is glorified by this: that you produce much fruit and prove to be My disciples.

As the Father has loved Me, I have also loved you. Remain in My love. If you keep My commands you will remain in My love, just as I have kept My Father's commands and remain in His love.

I have spoken these things to you so that My joy may be in you and your joy may be complete. This is My command: Love one another as I have loved you. No one has greater love than this, that someone would lay down his life for his friends. You are My friends if you do what I command you. I do not call you slaves anymore, because a slave doesn't know what his master is doing. I have called you friends, because I have made known to you everything I have heard from My Father. You did not choose Me, but I chose you. I appointed you that you should go out and produce fruit and that your fruit should remain, so that whatever you ask the Father in My name, He will give you. This is what I command you: Love one another." (John 15:1-17, HCSB)

Jesus is the life-giving vine. His love and righteousness are like the water and nutrients that are passed from the vine to the branches. We are his branches and the purpose of every follower of Christ is to produce fruit, lots and lots of luscious, delicious fruit. Branches will produce fruit, provided each one remains completely attached to the vine. What is the purpose of a branch? It was created to produce fruit. Every believer in Jesus was born from above, made to be a new creation. To be his disciple is to replicate his character. The fruit of the Spirit, which is his divine nature being slowly formed within us is: *love, joy, peace, patience, kindness, goodness, faithfulness, gentleness, and self-control* (Galatians 5:22-23a). Now read Jesus' teaching in John 15 one more time. Don't rush it.

Notice the brilliant way Jesus wove agapé love into the illustration of producing fruit. Keeping Jesus' commands is how we love him. This new command demands believers agapé love one another, just as Jesus loves them, *unconditionally*, warts and all. In this way, our lives will produce fruit that will last for all eternity. That fruit, my friend, is the impact and influence your life can have on other people. The impact is eternal because only the souls of boys and girls, teenagers, and men and women will remain forever. Your lasting fruit is about inspiring, encouraging, guiding, teaching, admonishing, and influencing people. Like Paul and his team, you can accomplish this by praying for yourself and everyone you lead. Jesus *appointed* you to produce righteous fruit that remains *"so that whatever you ask the Father in My name, He will give you."*

Will the Father answer our prayers to increase agapé love in the believers we lead? Of course, he will. Jesus knows that as long as we stay connected to him and remain in his love, we will be the kind of people who live the kind of lives that honor the Father. And there's nothing Jesus wants more than to honor his Father.

An outline of this prayer is on page 131. Tear it out and put it in your Bible or on your desk to help you remember to intercede in this way.

The final Kingdom Come Prayer has proven to be my absolute go-to prayer, especially in the heat of the moment.

Kingdom Come Prayer #3

Philippians 1:9-11

THE REQUEST

Dear Father, please make _____'s agapé love overflow more and more in full knowledge and complete discernment…

1ˢᵗ Result

so _____ can recognize the best choices today in every circumstance and interaction and be pure and blameless until the day of Christ…

2ⁿᵈ Result

so _____ can be filled with the fruit of righteousness that comes through Jesus Christ, to your glory and praise.

CHAPTER 6 – ASK FOR WISDOM & STRENGTH

The final Kingdom Come Prayer is the most practical to use throughout each day. I find myself flaring one of the two requests from this prayer on a continual basis – for myself and for those I'm privileged to influence. Some English translations interpret this prayer as one request. However, due to its close relationship with the two Ephesian prayers, it's more appropriately interpreted as two requests with multiple results.

For this reason also, since the day we heard this, we haven't stopped praying for you. We are asking that you may be filled with the knowledge of His will in all wisdom and spiritual understanding, so that you may walk worthy of the Lord, fully pleasing to Him, bearing fruit in every good work and growing in the knowledge of God. May you be strengthened with all power, according to His glorious might, for all endurance and patience, with joy giving thanks to the Father, who has enabled you to share in the saints' inheritance in the light. (Colossians 1:9-12, HCSB)

It is vitaly important to understand when Jesus taught his disciples how to pray, he taught them to ask for spiritual formation first (your kingdom come), and then to ask for physical needs next. Beginning your prayers by focusing on the Kingdom coming in the lives of those you lead will impact how you ask for their physical needs. Jesus explained so clearly in the Sermon on the Hill how his Father knows every specific need of his people (Matthew 6:19-34 and 7:7-11). Because of that fact, we're to stop worrying about physical needs so we can focus on the Kingdom coming first and foremost.

REQUEST #1 - Knowledge

We are asking that you may be filled with the knowledge of His will in all wisdom and spiritual understanding. (Colossians 1:9-12, HCSB) God wants his people to know his will for their lives. He longs for the *full* knowledge of his will to *fill* our minds and souls. He wants his people to *want* to know his will in the big decisions and the daily ones, too. To have confidence we can understand his will, we need his help. Being filled with the knowledge of his will is what happens when a follower of Jesus sets their heart and mind on the things above. The more we understand his will, the more we will realize our constant dependence on him. God's will is to give each of us more of his Spirit's influence within our spirit, so we'll grow in wisdom and understanding of his Word and his ways.

Doesn't it make sense our Father in the heavens wants us to know his will for our lives? Is he the kind of

Father who enjoys keeping us in the dark about his plans? Of course not! Since he *is* love, can he do anything other than communicate his desires to us as we ask him? Our steadfast Father wants nothing more than to lead his children to have unwavering love and devotion for him. Let's dig in further.

Knowledge of His Will

The request is *that you may be filled with the knowledge of his will in all wisdom and spiritual understanding.* (Colossians 1:9, HCSB) As we have discovered from the other Kingdom Come Prayers, the request is for a special kind of knowledge, a full and complete understanding of God and what he wants to happen. Paul was led to use this same Greek compound that he used repeatedly in the other Kingdom Come Prayers. This word depicts a full and complete comprehension and realization. The request goes even further. It is asking for a thorough knowledge of God's will in the specific circumstance or situation we're facing.

Do you know what challenges believers in your church are currently facing? What are their pressing needs? What are the issues they're wrestling with? What challenges are keeping them up at night? Life takes unexpected twists, tragedies happen, hopes are dashed, and we wonder why God didn't intervene as we expected. Knowing God's will for us can be very confusing, *if* we make it confusing. But our Lord most definitely does not want his people to be confused or anxious about knowing his will for their life. He wants us to understand how he communes with us, leading, guiding, and providing for us each day. As we live in the expectation of our Father revealing his will to us as we ask, we'll grow in our confidence of his direct involvement in our daily lives.

"I've Got This"

As a leader, how often have you neglected asking God to show you his will? Haven't you caused personal fender benders in ministry and life because you didn't ask, seek, or knock regarding what God wanted you to do? Isn't that true of everyone you lead? Haven't we all created unnecessary problems because we rushed in without asking God to guide us? It's so natural, even as a believer, to set a goal or pursue some desire and never consider how God might fit in to the equation. "I'll do it myself" is our human default. At our core, we tend to think, "I've got this." What we think we can do on our own ranges widely, from our to-do list for the day, to a career decision, to marrying a spouse or having children. Our default as humans is to figure it out on our own or to ask others *until* someone finally tells us what we want to hear.

Then a crisis hits, and we realize we don't have it figured out at all. Our plan wasn't the best way to go. This Kingdom Come Prayer request to know God's will can protect you, and everyone you lead, from making plans and setting goals without considering God's perspective. Imagine how much better life can be when the desire to know God's will rests in the forefront of a believer's thinking and planning? Wanting God's will more than personal plans is what being a disciple of Jesus Christ is all about. This is why Jesus told us: "*If anyone would come after me, let him deny himself and take us his cross daily and follow me. For whoever save his life will lose it, and whoever loses his life for my sake will save it"* (Luke 9:23-24). Following Jesus leads us toward becoming the kind of people who want to keep in perfect harmony with the melody our Father has written for us.

"As You Will"

This is precisely how Jesus prayed in the Garden of Gethsemane on that Holy Thursday night. The suffering he was about to endure was completely overwhelming to him. The anguish was so great Jesus' facial capillaries burst, *and his sweat became like great drops of blood falling down to the ground* (Luke 22:44). He repeatedly begged his Father for some other way: *And going a little farther he fell on his face and prayed, saying, "My Father, if it be possible, let this cup pass from me; nevertheless, not as I will, but as you will"* (Matthew 26:39).

Jesus was desperate. He begged his Father. He did not want to suffer and die on the cross. The word excruciating means "out of the cross." We cannot begin to fathom the spiritual suffering Jesus endured on our behalf. It was excruciating, but the spiritual suffering was so brutal Isaiah described it this way: *Just as many were appalled at You, His appearance was so disfigured, that He did not look like a man, and His form did not resemble a human being* (Isaiah 52:14, HCSB). Because he knew the intensity of his coming suffering, Jesus pleaded with his Father to divise some other way to redeem his people. He pleaded with his Father three times to remove this cup of suffering from him. He was in such emotional and spiritual distress that his Father sent an angel to strengthen him (Luke 22:43). And yet, because Jesus was completely devoted to his Father, his greatest desire was to be obedient. More than anything, he was going to honor his Father. Therefore, he prayed for his Father's will to happen instead of his own desires. In the midst of his tears and fears, Jesus wanted to do exactly as his Father had planned. He is our Lord and Savior, and he is our model of how to surrender our will to follow God's will.

The Father wants every follower of Jesus to become like his Son in his love and devotion. Of course, he wants to help in every way he can, giving all the guidance, wisdom, insight, and strength needed. Our part is to ask him persistently to give us the full knowledge of his will in every area of life and in every situation we face. He wants us to grow into the kind of people who long for his will to be the deciding factor, every time.

Knowing His Will

Knowing God's will is often thought of as a huge mystery. How can one be absolutely sure they understand his will in any given situation or decision? The Bible is very clear on many of life's choices. It is spelled out in black and white. However, each follower of Christ has many choices and decisions that are not spelled out so clearly in God's Word. "Should I pursue a promotion?" "Should I leave my company for this other position?" "Which home will be the best for us?" "What courses should I take this semester?" "Should I date Hannah or Mandy, or both?" "Should I replace my car?" "How much should I give to my church or to that family in need?" "Should we home-school?" "What should I do about serving in my church?" The daily questions they face can be overwhelming. The natural default to most of these questions is to try to figure it out on our own. Does God want to be involved in these decisions too? You better believe it! He is our Father in the heavens. He paid the ultimate price to purchase us from the domain of darkness. He knows every minute detail of every believer's life and he wants us to invite him into living life in an intimate relationship of dependence on him. You and your co-leaders can have a profound impact as you intercede in this way.

Spiritual Wisdom and Understanding

Our request is for God to fill those we lead with the full knowledge of his will *in all wisdom and spiritual understanding*. The Greek literally reads: "in all wisdom and understanding spiritual". "Spiritual" modifies both wisdom and understanding. Why isn't the word "spiritual" capitalized? Most English translators chose not to capitalize it because the context of the sentence conveys God is giving us wisdom and understanding within our spirits. It is our personal spiritual wisdom and understanding that is increasing, just as it is our personal love that is abounding in the Philippians 1:9 request. Because he lives in us, it is the Spirit of God who is giving us knowledge about the Father's will for us.

Who knows what's going to happen next year? Next week? Tomorrow? In the next two minutes? God does. The Spirit of God has all the knowledge and the know-how any follower will ever need. He knows everything about everything! Having him share his knowledge with us comes through the understanding and wisdom his Spirit reveals to our spirit. He gives insights about how to apply God's truth to specific situations, even when there isn't a go-to chapter and verse. The Spirit also brings to mind verses, passages, stories from the Bible, truths learned from sermons, books, and songs that guide us into understanding the will of God. The Spirit is always pointing his people to Jesus and the Father to help them understand life in the Kingdom.

The Process

Let's say someone in your church is facing a challenging situation and they don't know what to do. As you ask God, and keep asking him, to fill them with the knowledge of his will in all spiritual wisdom and understanding about what to do, *you* are already understanding his will. In the process of asking you are learning how to rely on God, which is his will for you and them. By reorienting your desire to want to know how to respond in a way that pleases God, you are living in the center of his will for your life, and you can give the proper guidance as needed. Even if in the end, you're not sure if they got it exactly right, as long as you sought the Lord's will through the process, you brought him great pleasure. How will it impact this person when you share that you've been diligently praying for them to understand God's will? Discerning God's answer about what is best to do or say is not always the end game. Learning to *rely* on him to understand his will is often the most important part of determining the will of God.

As Paul prayed for the believers in these churches, he also taught them how to pray for themselves. You can do the same. As you intercede for others, let them know how you are praying and encourage them to do the same. They can then learn how to depend on God for spiritual wisdom and insights. Together, you will both discover the knowledge of his will in all spiritual wisdom and understanding. You will both grow closer in your relationship to God and to each other. This is agapé love in action. This is how Kingdom leaders intercede.

Remember how Jesus ended the story that followed him giving the disciples the prayer outline? He concluded this very intimate time of teaching about prayer with this truth: *"If you then, who are evil, know how to give good gifts to your children, how much more will the heavenly Father give the Holy Spirit to those who ask him"* (Luke 11:13)? The only way to know the will of the Father is when his Spirit communicates it to our hearts and minds. Often the way he reveals his will is through our own Bible reading or by bringing certain verses to memory. There are obviously other ways as well. But the most important aspect of wanting the Kingdom to come in our lives is to ask God to fill us with the knowledge of his will in all spiritual understanding and all spiritual wisdom, and to keep on asking. He will do just as Jesus said and give us his Spirit to come along beside us to direct our steps.

Filled Up

Lastly, the prayer request is to be *filled* with the knowledge of God's will. To be filled up with the understanding of his will means there is no room for your own will, or her will, or their will. How often have we felt compelled to carry out someone else's plans? It sometimes feels like others are telling us: "God loves you, and *I* have a wonderful plan for your life." Being filled with God's will protects us from our own plans taking center stage and from being a puppet for someone else's desires.

Being filled with God's will means sin tendencies are being crowded out. If a leadership team is filled with the knowledge of God's will, there will be unity and confidence in their decisions. A church that is seeking a new pastor, or considering a building program, needs to be filled with the knowledge of God's will to prevent divisions and to ensure they are discerning together God's plans for them. The couple that is filled with the knowledge of God's will may have tensions and uncertainties about the decision they are making, but there will be unity and a sense of peace.

Have you noticed how easy it is to fill your mind and heart with all sorts of earthly things? Are you spending most of your mental energy thinking about future plans or challenges you're currently facing? Don't you think the same is true for everyone you lead? Worrying about children, aging parents, health, finances, investments, insurance, and retirement can easily snuff out joy and consume one's thinking. Our propensity is to be filled with the cares of this life. The busier our lives become and the more stuff we own, the more prone we are to have our time and attention focused on *things that are on earth*. We must work diligently at keeping our hearts and heads filled with the things that really matter, the eternal destiny of the people. Thoughts can be kept heavenward, and worry can be minimal, but only with God's help. Therefore, ask and keep on asking, seek and keep seeking, and knock and keep knocking.

1st Result – Worthy Walking

The first result of being filled with the full knowledge of God's will is: *so that you may walk worthy of the Lord, fully pleasing to Him* (Colossians 1:10a). In Jesus' day, to "walk" was a popular figure of speech to describe how people lived and conducted their lives. That is how it is used in this verse. You can replace "walk" with "live", if it makes more sense to you. Since the primary form of transportation in Jesus' day was walking, it's a perfect metaphor for living that dates back thousands of years, spanning the Old Testament period.

God wants us to live *worthy* of our calling. But the truth is none of us are worthy of being God's people. We don't deserve his mercy and forgiveness, not for a second. That's why it is called "grace". God gives us what we don't deserve because Jesus took upon himself what we did deserve, God's judgment for our sin-crimes. God's grace is working in us every day to help us think, say, and do what we would never have done on our own. He is constantly infusing his children with his Spirit's strength and wise influence. That is grace to live by. The most reasonable thing we can do is to ask God to fill us to the brim with the understanding of his will, so we can fall participate fully in his grace, living worthy of his calling.

For every attitude and action, worthiness can be evaluated with this question: Is this proper for someone who has been rescued and adopted by the Almighty? Imagine the impact of this question remaining in the forefront of a believer's thinking throughout the day. God wants to help his followers make life-choices that are worthy of Kingdom people. He is actively involved in our daily lives to renew our thinking and transform our behavior. He is leaning into us! Our Father fully expects we who have been given so much, will be actively involved in this renewal process. Our gratitude for all he has done, is doing, and will do, should compel us to want to live worthy of our calling. Praying these Kingdom Come Prayers is precisely how you can influence your church to participate fully in all God is doing in and through them. And that gives our Father great pleasure.

Making God Smile

To live worthy of the Lord means our choices are bringing him pleasure. Isn't it interesting that the Spirit added this phrase as another result, *fully pleasing to Him*? Thinking about how our thoughts, words, actions, and reactions impact Jesus is a very helpful way to stay in step with the Holy Spirit. Thinking about whether our decisions really please him keeps us in the center of his will. That's how we remain in him. We all become frustrated that even though the desire to please him is present, the will to pull it off is lacking, and we fail. Know that our Father is much more concerned about our *direction* than our perfection. It's about our heart's desires. That is why King David, who sinned in colossal ways, was called "a man after God's own heart."

How can those you shepherd make God smile? Ask him to fill them with the understanding of what he wants them to know and do. Ask him to give them recall of his Scriptures so they will obey his instructions in their daily decisions. This is how they will live lives that are worthy of the Lord and that truly please him.

2nd **Result - Bearing Fruit**

As you ask your Father to fill those you care for with the full knowledge of his will, *bearing fruit in every good work* (1:10b) will result. We explored the metaphor of fruit-bearing previously. But the wording in this verse is a bit different, so let's unpack it. Similar to the metaphor "to walk," "to work" is another word picture widely used in the Scriptures. Both metaphors are used in a powerful verse that should probably be memorized by all of Jesus' followers: *For we are his workmanship, created in Christ Jesus for good works, which God prepared beforehand, that we should walk in them* (Ephesians 2:10).

A good work is a good deed. Good deeds are not limited to actions but include words and thoughts. We are God's very workmanship, like a piece of art he is crafting, that has been created in Christ Jesus. One of the purposes for which we have been created in Christ is to serve others. The amazing thing is that our good deeds aren't just random acts of kindness. They were planned by God before we were ever born. This truth tells us that God is very intentional about what he wants us to do and say. That's why the phrase, "God has a plan for your life," has been so popular. It is true. God saved you from the dominion of darkness so you will do wonderful things for others that will have an eternal impact. He has placed you in the family, neighborhood, school, and vocation of his choosing so he can work in and through you to touch the lives of all with whom you have influence.

What if your teenager isn't making wise decisions? What if they love God but they just aren't really living for him? If their tree is full of leaves but little fruit, pray like crazy for the Father to fill them with the knowledge of his will in all spiritual wisdom and understanding. If those you're leading aren't *bearing fruit in every good work*, isn't it because they don't fully understand God's will for their life? They haven't grasped how their heavenly Father has things for them to do that will bring the fulfillment they are striving for in the wrong places. Ask and keep asking. Seek and keep seeking. Knock and keep knocking until your knuckles bleed.

You're Their Manure

Jesus told a captivating story about producing fruit. *And he told this parable: "A man had a fig tree planted in his vineyard, and he came seeking fruit on it and found none. And he said to the vinedresser, 'Look, for three years now I have come seeking fruit on this fig tree, and I find none. Cut it down. Why should it use up the ground?' And he answered him, 'Sir, let it alone this year also, until I dig around it and put on manure. Then if it should bear fruit next year, well and good; but if not, you can cut it down.'"* (Luke 13:6-9)

The first time I taught this passage, I told my church family that God brought me there to be fresh manure. My role was to help them grow so their lives would bear more fruit. Prayer is the key ingredient if you're going to successfully fertilize those you lead.

We are adored by the God of second chances, third chances, tenth chances, and on and on. God is digging around our trunk and adding manure to help us grow through our requests. This book is like that manure. My purpose is to help you grow so you can have a much greater Kingdom influence on every soul you lead. God wants to give his Spirit to help them produce all the fruit that he chose for them to yield. The wonderful thing about fruit production is that it is completely unique to each person, each family, each church, and each ministry. We can end the fruit comparison nonsense once and for all. Jesus made this point crystal clear in the story of the three servants in Matthew 25:14-30.

A man entrusted his property to his three servants and then left on a long journey. Each servant was given a different portion of his property to take care of *according to his ability*. (v15) This is a key phrase in the story. The man knew what his servants were capable of handling individually, so they were given responsibilities that aligned with their personal capabilities. God knows each of us very intimately, because he made us and gave us our unique abilities, skills, talents, opportunities, and giftedness. Stop worrying about what others are doing and focus on producing as much fruit in and through your life as you can. Avoid comparing your leadership effectiveness with someone else's. Always strive to do your best but leave the results up to God.

You have the opportunity to do the good works God chose for you to do every day. Good works are the plethora of opportunities you have every day to touch the life of another human. This is equally true of everyone you lead. Imagine your ministry or church if everyone was producing delicious fruit in *every resolve for good and every work of faith* (2 Thessalonians 1:11). It can happen as you and your fellow leaders pray diligently for every believer to be filled with the full knowledge of God's will in all spiritual wisdom and understanding. There's one additional result that will come to fruition as you pray this Kingdom Come Prayer.

3rd Result – More Growth

The final result from asking the Father to fill his people with the knowledge of his will is they will continue *growing in the knowledge of God* (1:10c). You guessed it. The word for knowledge is that same compound word used in v9 and that was used in every other Kingdom Come Prayer. The result of this request is the full and complete knowledge of God will be on the rise.

Isn't it amazing the God of the universe, Yahweh, who spoke everything into existence, wants us to know him fully and intimately? The more you ask for your church family to be filled with the understanding of what he wants them to say and do, the tighter their relationship with him becomes. If you think about it, it makes perfect sense.

What are you essentially requesting when you ask your Father to fill them with the knowledge of his will in all wisdom and spiritual understanding? *You* are living out your desperate dependence on God and acknowledging he knows everything about you and everyone you lead. By regularly asking God to guide them to understand his will about what they're facing, they will grow in their understanding of how he works, rightly applying his words and his ways. Isn't life in Christ all about learning just how desperately dependent we are on him?

Often times, we know exactly what the will of God is but lack the intestinal fortitude (guts) to do what we know is right. Of course, God doesn't want us to talk negatively about other people, but when the conversation goes that direction, we often can't seem to resist joining in. We know it is against God's will to look at porn, but the urge seems too strong to resist, and it's so readily available. At this point in the book, you've come to realize how much the Father wants to work through your prayers for his people, but you're just as busy as you were before you began reading it. What do you do?

REQUEST #2 - Strengthening

This Kingdom Come Prayer's second request is the one I pray the most, by far. I flare this request for myself and for those I lead multiple times, almost every day. As a Kingdom leader, this simple prayer request can radically enrich the righteous impact you have on others. *May you be strengthened with all power, according to His glorious might* (Colossians 1:11a, HCSB).

This request for power closely parallels the request in Ephesians 3:16. Paul's wording in the Ephesian prayer is more descriptive: *that according to the riches of his glory he may grant you to be strengthened with power through his Spirit in your inner being.* In the Colossian prayer, the apostle is much more direct, using exactly half the words to express the same need, to be empowered. You get the feeling he's in more of a hurry to get right to the central request. The poignancy and brevity of this powerful request is why I find myself repeating these words in the heat of the moment when there's an urgent need of the Lord's strength. It is a poignant flare prayer to launch heavenward when someone you lead is low on spiritual power. Of course, this request is just as applicable when you are spending longer times praying and using the Follower's Prayer Outline. Whether it's a flare or more, this request is praying according to the Father's will. Jesus promised his Father would most definitely answer every prayer that aligns with his will.

Multiple "Power" Words

As we have seen in these prayers, the apostle was so awestruck by the magnificence of the power of God that he used multiple words for "power" whenever he wrote about God's might. In this Colossian prayer, he asked for the believers to be *empowered* with all *power* according to God's *strength*. What can we learn from this special phrasing inspired by the Holy Spirit?

Our need for the Father to strengthen us is greater than what we can ever perceive. Our tendency, even as his redeemed people, is to revert back to the default attitude of most three-year olds, "I'll do it myself." We simply fail to recognize how much strengthening is needed in order for us to stand firm in our faith, resisting the world, the flesh, and the devil. To be strengthened with God's magnificent power will enable those you lead to stand firm in the strong winds of trials, disappointments, setbacks, and temptations. Through his power, they can live in the joy of their salvation even when it feels like all hell is breaking loose around them.

What is unique about this prayer request are the two results that come from it. These results help us to better understand how much of God's power we all need each and every day. It is these results that help us to grasp how critical it is that we persistently ask our loving Father to give us his power.

1st Result - Endurance and Patience

May you be strengthened with all power, according to His glorious might, for all endurance and patience (Colossians 1:11, HCSB). When you ask your heavenly Father to strengthen others, they will be empowered with all the endurance and all the patience needed for every circumstance and situation. What comes to your mind when you read *all endurance and patience*? What is someone you lead currently needing to push through? Who is trying their patience?

The quality and substance of our faith is tested every day. Stop and think about that. How was your faith tested yesterday? Did you stand firm in God's power? How did you endure that test? Did you rely on his strength in you? We all need his power to be able to endure life's trials and temptations as we patiently wait for the flood waters to subside.

My father-in-law endured treatment for larynx cancer. It was a horrible journey for him and his wife. Most of us know someone who has suffered through cancer treatment. The chemotherapy and radiation can produce side effects that make life almost unbearable. This is true for many other diseases as well. When we hear about someone being diagnosed with cancer, we immediately pray for healing, which is a loving thing to do. How do we pray for the Kingdom to come in the midst of cancer? There is no doubt our loving, heavenly Father calls for some to suffer great hardships in life, whether it comes from cancer, the tragic loss of a child or a spouse, financial ruin - the sources of suffering seem endless. However, we can be confident in knowing the will of God when suffering comes. God may choose to do something miraculous and suddenly end the pain. No matter what happens, he always wants to strengthen those who are suffering so they will have all the endurance and patience they need while at the same time never lose the joy of their place in his kingdom. His will is to empower us to persevere no matter how bad the circumstances are. This reality is what is described so passionately in Peter's two letters.

I vividly remember a past conversation with a young couple who had two small children. As the wife battled terminal cancer, they diligently looked for reasons why the Lord was allowing this illness. During treatments, they often had the opportunity to share with people the hope they had in Christ. Each conversation seemed to somehow justify their suffering. After many months of asking "Why Lord?", they accepted God's plan was not to heal her miraculously. His plan was to empower them to be able to patiently endure this trial while clinging to the joy of their salvation. They realized God had already done immeasurably more for them in giving them salvation than he could ever do in healing the cancer. Rescuing people from the domain of darkness is the greatest act of love God ever does for anyone. After months of treatments, the young woman went home to live with the Lord, while her husband and children remained steadfast in their faith.

Tough Times - Challenging People

A wonderful online Bible app is Blue Letter Bible. It defines endurance as "in the NT (New Testament) the characteristic of a man who is not swerved from his deliberate purpose and his loyalty to faith and piety by even the greatest trials and sufferings." Patience is a very close synonym. Both words can also be translated steadfastness, constancy, or endurance. The difference between these two words can be understood this way: endurance is what we need in tough circumstances and patience is what we need with trying people. That gives us a hook on which to hang these thoughts as we pray.

You and everyone you lead has and will continue to face many circumstances that will require endurance. You know exactly what that feels like. Jesus never promised to rid us of heartaches and hardships; he promised to remain with us in the middle of those trials. It is in the tough times of life we most need his enabling power. When the test shows it *is* cancer, when cutbacks are announced at work, and when insurance won't cover the damage, we need spiritual strength to endure. During the Covid-19 lockdown, we all needed every bit of endurance we could muster. Those who depended on the power of God to enable them to persevere were evident. When life is unfair, we need power from our Father to be able to persevere. God's power is there for the asking, to help his beloved people endure trials in order to know him better and better through the endurance.

We all have people in our lives who demand more patience than others. Marriage requires patience to endure and remain steadfast and true when the romance fades. If you have a middle schooler, you most definitely need enormous amounts of patience. The need for patience certainly doesn't fade as children become teens, it is simply a different *kind* of patience. So how do you show agapé love to someone who demands more patience than you have a prescription for? Ask your heavenly Father, and keep asking, to empower you with all power (you might want to capitalize ALL when you pray) according to his glorious power, so you can show the kind of patience that only comes from the Father's might.

As a Kingdom leader, I encourage you to make this your go-to prayer for yourself. If you are going to influence others towards Christlikeness, you most definitely need to be constantly empowered by God to have the patience and endurance you will need to run your race well. You need his power to pray for your church, just like Paul prayed for churches, so ask him and keep asking him. The Apostle persevered in his praying and you can too, as you make it a habit to ask the Father to strengthen you with all of his glorious might.

However, it's not a grit-your-teeth, white-knuckle kind of patient endurance that we are empowered with. When God is strengthening his children, endurance and patience are accompanied with joy.

2nd Result - Joy and Thanksgiving

May you be strengthened with all power, according to His glorious might, for all endurance and patience with joy giving thanks to the Father, who has enabled you to share in the saints' inheritance in the light. (Colossians 1:11-12, HCSB)

By God's power, the child of God is empowered to patiently endure with joy, not with anxiety or depression. This joy comes from the Spirit strengthening our heart and mind to realize our hope is in God and in him alone. He has chosen us by calling us out of the darkness and into his marvelous light. The Father decided to adopt us snotty-nosed, rebellious children, even though he knew we would not be as devoted to him as we should be. He has redeemed and forgiven us so we can all equally participate in the inheritance of the saints in the light of the kingdom of his dear Son.

The light of the Kingdom is the righteous radiance of the Son of God shining into our hearts and minds the fullness of God himself. The light of the Kingdom also points forward to the day when we will all have immortal bodies and live in the visible presence of Jesus and his Father, where there will be no need of a sun or moon because the radiance of their glory will be all the light we will need. (Revelation 21-22) Pretty cool, huh?

It is the Father himself who chose us and made us eligible. He enabled our adoption. We are qualified for the inheritance by God's grace and not because of anything we did or will do. Jesus was very clear that nothing can ever steal our eligibility in the Kingdom. Even our worst sins, if we are indeed in Christ, cannot disqualify us from the Kingdom. God has called us into his family; nothing can ever separate us from his love. A faith-fueling reminder of this fact is found in Romans 8:31-39.

It's easy to think about how much God loves his people. The challenge comes when we imagine God loving us personally, because we know all the junk that still resides within. This reality is true for everyone you lead. For many of us, we don't feel worthy of his love, but this is actually a good thing because we aren't. Therefore, we must rest in the power of his love because it is not dependent on our performance. Good works are never the source of forgiveness. They are the course of the forgiven. We do good deeds because God is making us good people, as he empowers us through his abiding Spirit. Enduring patiently with joy is impossible without the empowering strength of the Spirit of God within a soul. Realize this truth and change the way you live by asking God daily to strengthen you, and everyone you lead, with all power according to his glorious might. This is how the Kingdom will come in and through you, and them.

Spiritual Recharging

If someone is patiently enduring a tough challenge with little to no joy, ask your Father to strengthen them. When the joy of salvation is missing or running low, it's because their power supply is depleted. Their spiritual batteries are almost dead. The red bar is flashing. Do you recharge your cell phone every night? How much more does your spirit need recharging? The more you use your phone, the more frequently you need to recharge it. The more endurance, patience, and joy you need, the more you drain your spiritual power supply. Challenges require spiritual power. People who try our patience drain our spiritual batteries, especially those who require a lot of patience from us. Every temptation, discouraging remark, unloving response, or disrespectful email depletes our spiritual strength and drains our joy. Recharging our spirit is critically important. How do you do that? Pray. Pray at least as often as you charge your phone. I don't mean as long, but at least as frequently as you plug it in. That might not be a bad place to start if you are not in the habit of conversing with your Father each day.

If your leadership is fueled from occasional prayers or even a couple of flare prayers each day, you are missing out on the fullness of what God wants to do in and through you. Praying isn't about time, necessarily, but flare prayers must be coupled with times of quiet, reflective interaction with the Father and using the outline given to us by his Son. Being *strengthened with all power, according to his glorious might* often happens as you are praying and reading the Bible. The three Epistles we have been studying all have amazing passages that will renew your spiritual energy and equip you to face anything life might throw at you. Spending time reflecting on and praying through passages like John 6 and 15, Romans 7-8, Ephesians 1-2, Philippians 1-3, and Colossians 1-2 can bring you the renewed strength and encouragement that you need. God's word can ignite the desire and commitment to pray diligently for yourself and everyone you lead. Identifying favorite passages that rekindle your hope and reignite your joy will be one way the Father will renew your strength so you can patiently endure the hard stuff of life without losing your joy as a Kingdom leader.

Rescued and Redeemed

The two verses that follow the prayer are a rich example of why we should be joyful and grateful: *He has rescued us from the domain of darkness and transferred us into the kingdom of the Son He loves. We have redemption, the forgiveness of sins, in Him.* (Colossians 1:13-14, HCSB) Why do you think Paul was led to write such profound truths to conclude his prayer? The explanation is found within the passage. Studying the context of a passage is how we find the meaning of a verse or verses and learn how to apply them correctly to daily living. Let's look one more time at the context of this second request: *May you be strengthened with all power, according to His glorious might, for all endurance and patience, with joy giving thanks to the Father, who has enabled you to share in the saints' inheritance in the light. He has rescued us from the domain of darkness and transferred us into the kingdom of the Son He loves. We have redemption, the forgiveness of sins, in Him* (Colossians 1:11-14, HCSB).

Why do we give thanks to our Father? What is our source of joy? God has set us free! He sent his Son on the most dangerous rescue mission that has ever existed to save all of us, his people.

Jesus didn't suffer so we could be happy. Happiness is fleeting. Jesus' came to give us joy - his very own joy in us. Having his joy doesn't mean we are never sad or that life won't be difficult. Jesus wept at the tomb of his good friend Lazarus. He promised life will be hard in this world. Joy is much greater than happiness. Joy is the lasting emotion of knowing our place in God's kingdom is secure. That God is in absolute control of the galaxies, the nations, and our life, is the source of true joy. Joy comes from knowing God is with us, he will never leave us, and that he loves us just the way we are, warts and all. Joy grows as we realize how desperately dependent we are on our Father, for everything. He loves us so much he definitely won't leave us the way we are. He will grow us up in our faith, and that means we must persevere through the tough times. The joy of the Lord is knowing that we have been purchased for the Son, given to him as a most precious gift, and he will most assuredly see us safely home (John 6:35-40.

When your joy is replaced by worry and sadness, cry out to your Father to empower you with all strength according to his glorious power so you can know the full joy that is rightfully yours. Ask him, and keep asking him, to strengthen your mind and emotions to be able to overcome, by faith and with joy, your worries and sadness. Resolve in your heart that you want to know the joy of the Lord Jesus, and you want everyone in your church to see his joy in you. If you have determined to know his joy, you will diligently and consistently ask the Father to strengthen you with his power. The great news is that he will do it. Because God is faithful and he loves you with a steadfast love, he will strengthen you with all of his might for all the endurance and patience you will need as you face life's challenges. That endurance and patience with be coupled with the joy of the Lord, knowing you are his and nothing can ever change that reality.

Final Thoughts

Living in the strength of the Lord is tough to do. Living as a Kingdom leader in the strength of the Lord is even more difficult. That's why this fourth Kingdom Come Prayer from Colossians 1:9-12 is so strategic. As a leader, you need the Lord's wisdom and strength more than you will ever realize, at least on this side of eternity. Your church family trusts in you to help them grow towards maturity. The Father chose you to lead them in order for his kingdom to advance through your influence. He appointed you, in your leadership role, to help him bring about their sanctification.

If you are going to be the kind of Kingdom leader who impacts people on a level like Paul did, which is why God chose you, praying Paul's inspired prayers is essential. Your persistent praying will also inspire those to whom you are interceding. They will want to learn how pray like you do because they will experience the power of your prayers in their life. Encourage them to explore Kingdom Come Praying by using my book, *How to Ask God – For What He Wants to Give You*. That book, which is in paperback and audio formats, was written for every believer to learn Kingdom Come Praying while this book is dedicated to inspiring the Kingdom's leaders: pastors, bishops, ministers, directors, elders, and deacons. It's in paperback and audio formats.

On pages 163-164, you'll find the outlines of all four Kingdom Come Prayers. Tear this page out and keep them with you to remind you how to pray with Christ's words in you, in his name. The Father will answer every Kingdom Come Prayer you pray. This is Jesus' promise. Let that reality inspire you to prioritize the work of interceding for yourself, your family, your co-leaders, leaders in government, and everyone in your church or ministry.

> *Now to Him who is able to protect you from stumbling and to make you stand in the presence of His glory, blameless and with great joy, to the only God our Savior, through Jesus Christ our Lord, be glory, majesty, power, and authority before all time, now and forever. Amen.* Jude 24-25 HCSB

Kingdom Come Prayer #4

Colossians 1:9-12

REQUEST #1

Father, please fill me with the full knowledge of your will in all wisdom and spiritual understanding…

1st Result

so that the way I live will be worthy of you, fully pleasing you in every way…

2nd Result

so that I will produce fruit in every good thing I think, say, and do…

3rd Result

so I'll continue to grow in my knowledge of you.

REQUEST #2

And strengthen me with all power according to your glorious might…

1st Result

for all endurance and patience…

2nd Result

with joy, I'll thank you for making me eligible to share in the inheritance of the saints in light.

Kingdom Come Prayer #1 Ephesians 1:17-19

THE REQUEST I ask you, the glorious Father of my Lord Jesus Christ, to give those I lead your Spirit who has all wisdom and revelation, to help them know you more fully, having my heart flooded with your light…

1ˢᵗ Result

> so they will know the hope of your calling…

2ⁿᵈ Result

> so that they will know the riches of your glorious inheritance in the saints…

3ʳᵈ Result

> so that they will fully comprehend the greatness of your power that's available to all who believe.

Kingdom Come Prayer #2 Ephesians 3:16-19

THE REQUEST Dear Father in the heavens, I ask that out of your glorious riches you will grant the saints that I lead to be strengthened with your power through your Spirit in my inner most being…

1ˢᵗ Result

> so you, Lord Jesus, will be more at home in their hearts through faith, making them rooted and grounded in agapé love…

2ⁿᵈ Result

> so they'll have strength together to understand how wide and high and long and deep your love is Jesus, experiencing it beyond knowledge…

3ʳᵈ Result

> so together, they'll be filled with all of your fullness.

Kingdom Come Prayer #3 Philippians 1:9-11

THE REQUEST Dear Father, please make _____'s agape love overflow more and more in full knowledge and complete discernment...

1ˢᵗ Result

so _____ can determine recognize the best choices today in every circumstance and interaction and be pure and blameless until the day of Christ...

2ⁿᵈ Result

so _____ will be filled with the fruit of righteousness that comes through Jesus Christ, to your glory and praise.

Kingdom Come Prayer #4 Colossians 1:9-12

REQUEST #1 Father, fill me with the full knowledge of your will in all wisdom and spiritual understanding...

1ˢᵗ Result

so that the way I live will be worthy of you, fully pleasing you in every way...

2ⁿᵈ Result

so that I will produce fruit in every good work

3ʳᵈ Result

so I'll continue to grow in my knowledge of you.

REQUEST #2 Strengthen me with all power according to your glorious might...

1ˢᵗ Result

for all endurance and patience...

2ⁿᵈ Result

with joy, I'll thank you for making me eligible to share in the inheritance of the saints in light.

My Adventures

I never imagined becoming a pastor. I actually rejected the idea for several years. My first foray into church leadership was in my late twenties, as an elder in a dynamic, mainline denominational church. As a leadership team, we had the momentous task to determining if our historic church would remain in a denomination that was rapidly abandoning its evangelical roots or continue to try and be a light in the darkness. At the same time, we were in negotiations with PTL and Jim Bakker to purchase their original property as our new church location. Needless to say, my first years in church leadership, as a volunteer, were full of important life-lessons. A few years later, after completing seminary studies, I went on to become the field director of a missionary team in the Muslim country of Senegal, West Africa. We lived there six years, until our next adventure in ministry, serving as the senior pastor of our sending church. In the subsequent nine years, the church grew from 350 to over 1,300 worshippers while I simultaneously faced numerous hardships and heartaches, including two church coup attempts. But that's vocational ministry, right? My final pastorate was to shepherd a small, fledgling church. By God's grace and with the help of some very fine elders, the church grew healthy and strong. If I could go back to make one change in each of these ministry roles, it would be to make intercession, using the Kingdom Come Prayers, my absolute priority.

In addition to the vocational ministry roles described above, I have been privileged to have owned two businesses, worked for two Fortune 100 firms, three smaller companies, and launched a nonprofit organization. God has used all of these experiences to instill within me a passion to bring clarity and instill confidence in the people of God, especially his devoted shepherds who work so tirelessly. You can discover additional resources on my website, www.BillSimpson.org.

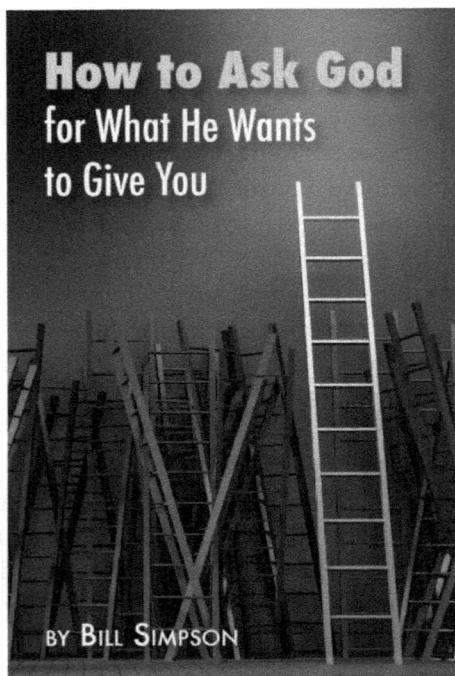

How to Ask God for What He Wants to Give You
BY BILL SIMPSON

How to Ask God brings a fresh and easy-to-read perspective on praying. It is a more expanded and detailed version of **Kingdom Come Leadership.** This book teaches, directly from the Bible, how God wants you to pray, and what he wants you to ask him to do. Jesus taught that if we remain in him and his words remain in us, we can ask for whatever we want, and it will happen! Learn how Jesus' promise can become your daily experience. It's an excellent resource for small groups and Bible studies, as well as an engaging devotional for couples. Each chapter concludes with five discussion questions. A free Leader's Guide is also available on the website. You can purchase the book at Amazon or any online book retailer or through HowtoAskGod.com.

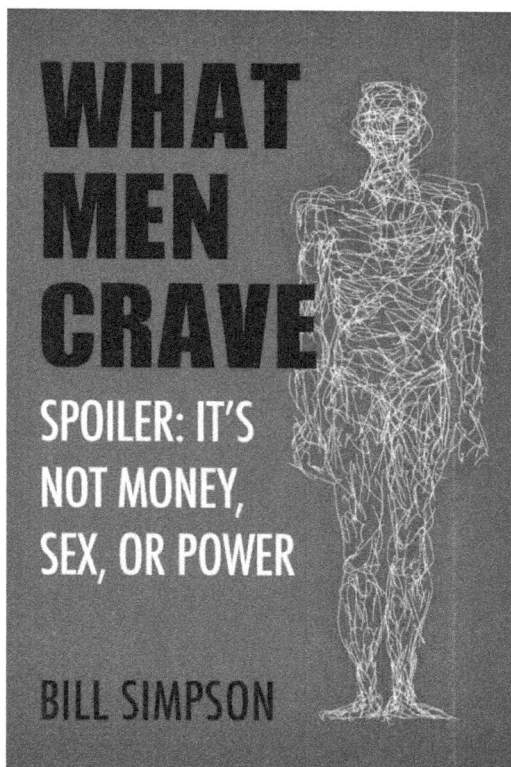

What Men Crave is a guidebook into the deepest needs of every man, his RAH cravings: Respect, Admiration, and Honor. The book will inspire confidence and instill clarity within you about how you are wired and how you were created to be a man of God – a truly honorable man. Through scientific and biblical research, you will discover how to better understand yourself, the men you work with, and the man you married. A free audiobook is available with the purchase of a paperback or an eBook, and it's on Audible.

Take 10 to Menó
10 MINUTE DAILY READINGS THRU COLOSSIANS

"Those who remain (menó) in me, and I in them, will produce much fruit. For apart from me, you can do nothing."
~Jesus Christ

Bill Simpson

Bill's third book is the first of a series of devotional books called **Take 10 to Menó – 10 Minute Daily Readings thru Colossians**. The Greek word "menó" means to "abide", "remain", and "continue." Jesus taught his followers must remain in his teachings if they are to truly continue following him as their Lord. The first book in this series takes the reader through the letter to the Colossians in eighteen, ten-minute devotional readings. A free blog of this book is available on Bill's website at www.BillSimpson.org/take-10-blog-page.

Drive
Time
Devotionals
with Bill Simpson

Drive Time Devotionals is a podcast of practical and applicable biblical teaching by Bill. Each episode is about 10 minutes long, just right for your commute to work or your time on the treadmill. Feed your heart, mind, and soul through Bill's delightful, and thoroughly biblical, teaching. You can listen to the podcast on iTunes, Spotify, Google Play, or Sketcher.

www.ingramcontent.com/pod-product-compliance
Lightning Source LLC
Chambersburg PA
CBHW060320050426
42449CB00011B/2577